REACHING
UNCHURCHED TEENS

YOUTH MINISTRY IN THE TRENCHES

01057674

REACHING
UNCHURCHED TEENS

YOUTH MINISTRY IN THE TRENCHES

★ ★ ★ ★ ★

Rick Bundschuh

Standard®
PUBLISHING
Bringing The Word to Life

Cincinnati, Ohio

Published by Standard Publishing, Cincinnati, Ohio
www.standardpub.com

Copyright © 2009 by Rick Bundschuh

Also available from the Youth Ministry in the Trenches series: *Building & Mobilizing Teams* and *Engaging Parents as Allies*

Printed in the United States of America

Project editor: Robert Irvin
Cover and interior design: Thinkpen Design, Inc., www.thinkpendesign.com

Series contributor: David Olshine

All Scripture quotations are taken from the Holy Bible, NEW INTERNATIONAL VERSION®. NIV®. Copyright © 1973, 1978, 1984 by International Bible Society. Used by permission of Zondervan. All rights reserved.

Scripture quotations marked *The Message* are taken from The Message by Eugene H. Peterson. Copyright © 1993, 1994, 1995, 1996, 2000 by NavPress Publishing Group. Used by permission. All rights reserved.

ISBN 978-0-7847-2315-9

Library of Congress Cataloging-in-Publication Data

Bundschuh, Rick, 1951-
  Reaching unchurched teens / Rick Bundschuh.
    p. cm. -- (Youth ministry in the trenches)
  ISBN 978-0-7847-2315-9
  1. Church work with teenagers. 2. Missions. I. Title.
  BV4447.B778 2009
  259'.23--dc22
                                    2009018016

CONTENTS

WITH TRUTH AND RELEVANCE

I like unbelievers. Sometimes I like them more than I do believers. I especially like unbelievers who become believers. These characters, if not squeezed into the cookie-cutter mold of some tired version of Christianity, often bring a fresh perspective, exuberance, and even a sense of questioning that the church needs to stay on her toes. They spot the self-righteous in a heartbeat and, at least initially, are not afraid to question apparent injustices or inconsistencies. These are among the reasons I'm so passionate about translating the ancient and timeless truths of the Christian faith into the vernacular of our modern culture. We must reach unbelievers with truth and relevance.

For some reason, I've been fairly good at this kind of thing. My first full-time position outside of my home church was as a middle school youth pastor. I had eleven church kids in the group to start with. A year and a half later my weeknight meetings were running past three hundred students, but only eleven of them were "church kids."

I had limited help and even fewer resources. The experience was both nutty and exhilarating. God did wild things then, and continues to do wild things now, as some of those seeds cast long ago have taken root.

Eventually, I came to Hawaii and, with a group of other spiritual lunatics, started a church for people who didn't particularly like going to church. Around 85 percent of our congregation (children, youth, and adults) was not raised in Christian homes. This makes things really interesting when you ask them to find a book in the Bible. (I have watched them thumb backwards while looking for Genesis.)

The concepts and tips in this book come from many years of doing youth work that has a heavy emphasis on reaching little pagans. There are many practical ideas and some philosophical points for you to chew on.

However, there is no universal template for reaching the unchurched. I don't think one exists, and if some publisher tries to sell one to you, don't believe it. There are generalities and "works much of the time"-type ideas, but I have seen effective outreach violate virtually every one of the things I declare as precepts in this book. I've discovered that God is not at all limited to our well-devised plans and strategies.

To be honest, in a number of places where I did ministry, I had more than a hard time once the unbelieving hordes began to invade the youth group. I often swung between joy and discouragement, along with a large helping of confusion, as I watched Christians react in varying ways to the good news being spread to the unreached. What kept me going was the firm conviction that this is the will of God.

I believed that then, and I believe it now.

God loves the trolls, varmints, cretins, and unwashed heathens. He loves the left-wing loonies, the raging, right wing zealots—and even the nutty electrician who, while wiring my house, told me in all seriousness and in hushed tones about the reptilian space invaders cloaked as politicians and world leaders that were preparing to rule the earth. (It was all I could do to keep a straight face during our conversation, and I have to confess that I laughed out loud for some time after he left!)

I want to love what God loves. I think you do too. Otherwise, you wouldn't have picked up this little book. My hope is that those in your church share this love as well—not just in word, but in being open to Jesus changing the very nature of their community with a flood of new people who are everything they are not.

May God use you as his catalyst, his vehicle, his mirror—as you love those the Son died to save. Including, yes, even those who believe in reptilian invaders.

Dedication

Almost everyone who finds the narrow path does so because someone, in harmony with the Holy Spirit, acted as a signpost in that direction. These are often family members or close friends whose faith is not just spoken but lived. On occasion a totally unrelated person bobs up unexpectedly and becomes the instrument of God in our lives. And on rare occasions that person becomes not only a signpost but also a mentor and model. In my journey from paganism to the cross, that sign-holder, mentor, model, and friend was E.G. Von, an unsung but revolutionary youth worker.

The ideas in this book were first modeled for me by his work. But frankly, I also owe a lot to the churches I have served in and, in particular, some of the leadership staff who winced, prayed, swallowed hard, and risked much, gambling that the crazy stuff their young youth worker was always cooking up would not end up costing them their job or a lawsuit—or both.

They looked the other way while messes were made, vans trashed, money spent, and kids prowled where they shouldn't have been.

I greatly appreciate the vote of confidence from all of you and it is to you that I dedicate this little work.

Rick Bundschuh

KAUAI, HAWAII

PART ONE

THINKING IT THROUGH

THINKING THROUGH WHY WE DO THIS

Call me naive, call me ignorant, call me idealistic—but I honestly believed the church's search committee when they said that one of the goals they had for the new middle school youth ministry position they were creating was to have evangelism take place among young people. Perhaps we were talking past each other and agreeing to very different things when they hired me for my first youth ministry job outside my home church. Perhaps what they were envisioning was a small trickle of smartly dressed honor students entering the kingdom of God and finding its way to the front row of the church through the efforts of this new youth ministry.

What they got was something completely different.

They got swearing, brawling, profane, self-centered kids from broken homes in the shady part of town. They got little toughs that threatened some of the kids and flipped the bird at the women who tried to scold them for speeding past them on their skateboards. In short, they got the youth world's version of the barbarian hordes.

I thought the people on the church board would be happy. If anyone needed to hear the good news of Jesus, it was these kids. Most of them had never held a Bible in their hands until they showed up at youth group. Few had used the name of Jesus in any way other than as part of a curse. Hardly any had ever been to Sunday school or heard any of the Old Testament Bible stories. They were, in spiritual terms, blank slates.

I thought that the church parents would be excited to see so many new faces. Some of them were, but a number were less than enthusiastic. As the count of newbies outstripped the old-timers, the parents became even less enamored with what was going on.

"They'll be a bad influence on my child," one said.

"These are the kinds of kids I send my son to church to get away from," said another.

Surely the pastor and other staff members will have my back, I thought.

The pastor invited me into his office and encouraged me to expose the kids to classical music and other cultural things while we were sharing the gospel. (I considered it a victory just to add some Christian rock tunes to the collection of X-rated tunes they were already listening to.) He was older, nearly ready to retire, and out of touch with what was happening in the middle school ministry of the church.

The janitor was upset because of the toilet paper ceiling decorations that were appearing in the bathrooms. The financial guys started to grouse about the amount of money being spent on sodas, toys, props, gas, and other items typical of a youth ministry that is growing in big ways, and with regularity. A number of people groused under their breath that these kids were coming just to be entertained and that the gospel was obviously not being preached.

Meanwhile, more and more kids were showing up—terrorizing the neighbors, smoking cigarettes behind the Dumpster, and even a few sporting apparel that made hookers look tame. Their clothes created some interesting contrasting statements. (My memory of the kid sitting and reading the Bible while wearing a T-shirt with a huge pot leaf on it is still vivid. I should have photographed it.)

Teens were coming to Christ right and left. Their young lives were slowly coming under the influence of the Word. But I had them for only a couple of hours a week and the world had them the rest of the time, so it was slow going with a lot of the two-steps-forward/three-steps-back dance going on. There were moments of glory and moments of youth work horror—like the time I had a big bully of a kid who wanted to start a brawl with me right in the middle of youth group because I asked him to please quiet down and participate.

The church got what the members said they wanted. They had unsaved teens coming out their ears and new entries into the kingdom of Heaven every week.

But they did not like what they got.

Some board members called for my termination. I was thunderstruck, confused, hurt. How could this be? I had beaten the bushes to find these little unbelievers and spent huge amounts of time investing in these kids! How could anyone think this was anything but glorious?

Ah, but I was so wrong.

Before long the church board was battling over my job with a slim margin winning the "keep the lad" vote at each monthly meeting. I was on pins and needles while the church divided into "reach out" and "protect our own" camps.

I was learning the lesson that even though people say they want something, they may not like it if they actually get it.

I ended up leaving the church on my own. The reason? They could say they wanted evangelism, but when it came right down to it, they could not do it or tolerate it being done.

TRUTH FROM THE TRENCHES

When it comes to evangelism, some corners of the church may say they want outreach, but may not like it if they actually get it.

WHATEVER IT TAKES

This book is for people who truly want to reach the kids hanging out at the neighborhood skate park or mall. It's for those who have a heart for the lost boys who feast on cyberporn and the dolled-up girls who have given away their bodies too easily and too young. It's for those with a high tolerance for unsaved kids who swear because swearing is the language of the world in which they live and breathe. This book is for those who are willing to step in to become a mentor or surrogate uncle/aunt/older sibling to kids who go home to half a family. Or for those who have no idea what it's like to go to sleep without a pillow wrapped around your head to block out the fighting and screaming—but who want to be there, completely and like Jesus, for those who do.

This book is for those who are willing to do whatever it takes to reach the many who are hurting in these ways.

This book has the potential to be a bit dangerous as well. Successfully attract a bunch of rogues and you may find out how much your church really wants wholehearted evangelism. You may find your youth group rebelling at the change in pecking order, your parents up in arms about the invasion of the nasty kids, and your coworkers alarmed at the ill-mannered behavior of those wild teens.

You may find unexpected conflict flaring up. You may find the way you teach changing. You may find your expectations altering. You may find your heart breaking. And you may find the joy of seeing and being part of the greatest miracle of all: a changed life both now and for eternity.

Which, of course, is why we do this.

We roll up our sleeves and plunge into the dingy youth culture that rages outside the walls of the church not just because we are told by our Master that we must, but because of the joy that comes from seeing a lost sheep found, a crumpled soul unfolded, and a broken heart healed.

For me, all these ideas are quite personal. I was once one of those unwashed outsiders for whom Christian jargon was a mystery, and for whom the idea of going to church was equal to signing up for a torture session with a water board. But an innovative youth worker with strong backing from his church pulled me off the beach for an activity that at the time seemed like anything but outreach—a surfing trip to Mexico. That trip cemented my friendship with the youth worker, gave me my first understandable taste of the gospel, and ultimately led to putting my faith in Christ a year and a half later.

When I decided to do for others what had been done for me by becoming a full-time youth worker, I simply modeled the effective methods of connecting with unreached kids that had worked so well with me.

Many years have passed since I was the curious, lanky, suntanned kid being wooed by the message of Christ. But through the decades I have continued to look for ways to connect with and become friends with unbelievers and, if God allows, to tell of the hope that is within me.

LOVING OTHERS . . . JUST BECAUSE

People do outreach for a lot of reasons. Here are just a few scenarios:

- ★ Some are on an evangelical jihad and driven more by a sense of mission than anything else. The people they meet are targets, souls to be saved.
- ★ Some people do outreach out of obligation. They know that a Christian is supposed to pass on their faith, so in order to be obedient to Christ they slog along with their outreach plan.
- ★ Some people share Christ with a burst of enthusiasm that comes from their new experience with him, but often find their efforts to tell others cooling as they settle into the rugged rhythm of living like a Christian.

God can and does use just about any method, or even motive, devised by humans to get his message out. (Philippians 1:15-18 is a great passage to reference on this point.) But that does not mean that those methods or motives are the best for our souls or those we are reaching out to.

While this is a book with a lot of method ideas in it, those methods are predicated on the youth worker actually having a heart that is willing to love teens regardless of whether they respond to the message of Christ or not. These are not to be seen as gimmicks to increase attendance but ideas on how to connect your heart and the hearts of your coworkers with the hearts of those outside the family of Christ. These are ideas, helps, and tips that can give you the permission to speak into the life of a teen and become his or her friend. They need to be used with that particular vision in mind.

TRUTH FROM THE TRENCHES

To reach the unchurched, you must have a heart that is willing to love teens regardless of whether they respond to the message of Christ or not. You cannot go after gimmicks to increase attendance but instead must go after the hearts of those outside the family of Christ.

THE NEED

Theologians are fond of saying that we live in a post-Christian culture. What they mean is that a growing number of North Americans (and Europeans, who reached this point years before us) no longer consider themselves as distinctly Christian or think and process morals and ethics through a Christian or biblical filter.

In past decades, claiming allegiance to a faith and putting in an occasional appearance at the neighborhood house of worship were politically correct, even if for all practical purposes you weren't truly a believer. At least in that kind of society you had a thin icing of religiosity, with most claiming "Christian" as their favorite flavor. Regardless of how people acted, they would at least give lip service to a broad range of Christian-based morality and ethics (with some notable exceptions, such as bigotry).

Today we have a huge swath of parents (whether one or two in the household) that no longer has a Christian impulse nor feels the need to subscribe to biblical ethics, standards, and values. They make up their own value system or adopt a smorgasbord approach that allows them to pick and choose from the Christian-based values that they are OK with and ignore the ones they find distasteful.

Few of these parents feel the need to imprint spirituality on their children by sending them off to Sunday school. In fact, many are ambivalent about the whole issue of a spiritual heritage for their children, declaring that the kids "can decide for themselves if they want to believe in God or choose a religion when they are older." The offspring of those parents are spiritually adrift children who have no anchors to give them boundaries and no solid context to make proper choices in life.

And these parents are alongside the many, many parents who do want the best for their children spiritually, but don't know how, or lack the confidence, to effectively lead them.

It is this world that we are called to speak into.

TRUTH FROM THE TRENCHES

Today we have a huge swath of parents that no longer has a Christian impulse nor feels the need to subscribe to biblical ethics, standards, and values.

THE IDEAL TIME AND AGE GROUP FOR EVANGELISM

The teen years—and the early teen years in particular—are pivotal for introducing an unbeliever to Jesus Christ. Finding listening ears and open hearts is far easier during this time of life than any other, yet Christian communities often miss or ignore the opportunity.

Suppose you are into fishing. I don't mean that you simply enjoy a trip to the wilderness, reveling in the scenery, and basking in the solitude while trying to snatch a trout or two in the process. I mean you are really into fishing, with the goal of coming home with as many fish as you can hook. Suppose you had a few fishing spots to choose from. In some locations your odds of catching a fish are quite low, but in one particular fishing pond, your odds are quite high. Where do you go fishing? The answer for a hard-core fisherman is obvious. You go to the time-tested spots where, over and over, you find yourself catching more fish.

TRUTH FROM THE TRENCHES

Finding listening ears and open hearts is far easier for those working with teens and, especially, early teens, yet Christian communities often miss or ignore the opportunity.

For years, survey after survey has shown that the majority of people who become Christians make that decision sometime before they leave their teens (estimates are as high as 85 percent), with a large percentage of commitments made before ninth grade. The same studies show that as a person ages the statistical probabilities of him or her coming to Christ become less and less. So the teen years represent a prime fishing hole, one in which many who are called to be fishers of men should be working, especially if they're serious about catching fish, not merely being recreational fishermen.

Using simple logic, any church that is truly concerned about seeing souls come to a saving knowledge of Jesus Christ should be spending a great deal of its time, energy, and resources toward this age group, where there is such a high potential for response. Although many in church leadership are aware of these facts, very little energy is spent making the most of this opportunity. Little skilled manpower, thought, money, or resources are focused toward the middle school (approximately eleven to fourteen) age levels.

In the community of faith where I serve as teaching pastor, coming to grips with this reality altered the rhythm of how we do ministry. Our key evangelical point man is our middle school youth pastor. Our church spends a great deal of its resources making sure that the tools and personnel are in place for the evangelism of this age group. Should there be a financial crisis where staff cuts are necessary, the middle school youth worker has as much or more job security as anyone on staff—he would be the last man standing and the last ministry to feel the ax. So vital is this fishing pond that it takes priority over most every other evangelical effort given importance by the church.

Youth workers, we may need to sharpen our focus and energy toward the teens and preteens who roam the neighborhoods, skate parks, and malls. What is quite clear is that an introduction to Christ at this point in maturity often, and obviously, gets results.

ACTION PLAN

★ Where have you seen evangelism wanted in word but not in deed? Are there ways you can grow your heart toward the previously unreached?

THINKING THROUGH THE MODELS OF JESUS AND THE EARLY CHURCH

One of the reasons I've never become hopelessly discouraged, in spite of the obvious lack of enthusiasm some Christians and even church leaders have for chasing after the rough-edged kinds of lost kids, is that I know the impulse to reach the down and dirty is in rhythm with the heartbeat of Jesus. Everything I know about our Lord shows that he revels in loving the rawest of the raw, and he is not fazed by predictable results from the holier-than-thou types. A quick perusal of the gospels shows that Jesus was so willing to mix it up with the dregs of society that he consistently outraged the religious professionals and often confused his strongest supporters.

THE PRECEDENT

You may recall that John the Baptist, obviously concerned with the rumors he had been hearing about Jesus partying with undesirables, sent some of his followers to check things out; they were armed with a curious question. "When John heard in prison what Christ was doing, he sent his disciples to ask him, 'Are you the one who was to come, or should we expect someone else?'" (Matthew 11:2, 3). The question is so loaded you can almost read between the lines—so here's an attempt to do so. I'll call this Rick's expanded, slightly imaginative, and youth worker-friendly version: "Uh, we hear that, unlike our ascetic master John, you're at all the rowdy parties in town and making friendly with the scabbiest sorts of people—and you've even been spotted sipping a wine cooler now and then. So we've been sent to ask: are you really the One we are expecting or, um . . . uh, should we check out somebody else?"

And I love the response that Jesus hands those boys to take back to John: "Go back and report to John what you hear and see. . . . Blessed is the man who does not fall away on account of me" (Matthew 11:4, 6).

> Jesus replied, "Go back and report to John what you hear and see: The blind receive sight, the lame walk, those who have leprosy are cured, the deaf hear, the dead are raised, and the good news is preached to the poor. Blessed is the man who does not fall away on account of me."
>
> MATTHEW 11:4-6

Let's do the math on this. Hang out with a bunch of no goods while truly making it your goal to love and impact them like Jesus did, and you'll set tongues wagging and rumors flying to the point that people will question your methods, your ethics, and even your calling. But you may also get a boatload of miracles and changed lives.

If John was a bit confused, he was in good company. Even the guys who signed on as disciples of Jesus were befuddled at the people he chose to hang out with. One day, for example, they ran into the nearby town to get some food. When they got back, to their surprise they found that Jesus was in a full-blown discussion with a local floozy. They had to muster all the control they could to not blurt out something like, "Who the heck is this chick, and why are you giving her the time of day?" (See John 4:27.)

But the people who Jesus really drove nuts were the religious guys who prided themselves on just how much distance they could put between themselves and the slimy sinners. Over and over again they would wag their fingers at his choice of dinner companions or grumble in hushed tones about the stained reputation of some character with whom Jesus was hanging out.

And time and time again Jesus would explain his mission to them: "Jesus, overhearing, shot back, 'Who needs a doctor: the healthy or the sick? I'm here inviting the sin-sick, not the spiritually fit'" (Mark 2:17, *The Message*).

He even tried to get his point across in clever parables such as the story of the king's wedding banquet, found in Matthew 22:1-10, which illustrated perfectly that the religious weren't truly interested in God's invitation—but the seemingly unfit were.

Jesus spoke to them again in parables, saying: "The kingdom of heaven is like a king who prepared a wedding banquet for his son. He sent his servants to those who had been invited to the banquet to tell them to come, but they refused to come. Then he sent some more servants and said, 'Tell those who have been invited that I have prepared my dinner: My oxen and fattened cattle have been butchered, and everything is ready. Come to the wedding banquet.'

"But they paid no attention and went off—one to his field, another to his business. The rest seized his servants, mistreated them and killed them. The king was enraged. He sent his army and destroyed those murderers and burned their city.

"Then he said to his servants, 'The wedding banquet is ready, but those I invited did not deserve to come. Go to the street corners and invite to the banquet anyone you find.' So the servants went out into the streets and gathered all the people they could find, both good and bad, and the wedding hall was filled with guests."

MATTHEW 22:1-10

THE EARLY CHURCH

The precedent set by Jesus was most fully followed in the early church not by the original disciples, but by the apostle Paul. He plowed deep furrows outside the small and contained Jewish world and flooded the church with individuals who shared none of the Hebrew background—culturally or morally. Nor did they have the messianic thinking common to Jewish beliefs.

Fights would break out among the early believers over the seemingly most innocent of issues—serving up meat bought at a bargain because it had been roasted on the altar of some phony Roman god; or whether a new male believer, who was not a Jew, should be asked to mark himself as Jews did by undergoing physical circumcision. The correspondence from Paul is full of hints and instructions about these kinds of petty squabbles. But even though the church at times displayed marked adjustment problems to the new outside blood, Paul set sail—with maniacal joy—all around the Roman empire, adding many more rare birds to the kingdom of Heaven at nearly every port.

And, as is true whenever you really mix it up with the world, the influx of the rawest of the raw created—and still creates—a lot of trouble. In Acts 16:16-24, Luke narrated a sample incident that took place in the bustling town of Philippi:

Once when we were going to the place of prayer, we were met by a slave girl who had a spirit by which she predicted the future. She earned a great deal of money for her owners by fortune-telling. This girl followed Paul and the rest of us, shouting, "These men are servants of the Most High God, who are telling you the way to be saved." She kept this up for many days. Finally Paul became so troubled that he turned around and said to the spirit, "In the name of Jesus Christ I command you to come out of her!" At that moment the spirit left her. (continued p.27)

When the owners of the slave girl realized that their hope of making money was gone, they seized Paul and Silas and dragged them into the marketplace to face the authorities. They brought them before the magistrates and said, "These men are Jews, and are throwing our city into an uproar by advocating customs unlawful for us Romans to accept or practice."

The crowd joined in the attack against Paul and Silas, and the magistrates ordered them to be stripped and beaten. After they had been severely flogged, they were thrown into prison, and the jailer was commanded to guard them carefully. Upon receiving such orders, he put them in the inner cell and fastened their feet in the stocks.

ACTS 16:16-24

SLAUGHTERED SACRED COWS

What happened in Philippi was that someone's sacred cow got slaughtered—in this case, the money-making potential of the little fortune teller. People are often less than enthusiastic about seeing rough-around-the-edges new blood enter the church because they're afraid they'll have to make changes they don't care for or face problems they don't want to deal with.

And what they fear is true. People from rough-and-tumble backgrounds bring with them all their bad habits, poor decision-making abilities, damaged souls, and twisted thinking.

However, the church belongs to Jesus, not to any particular interest group. If Jesus wants to change a middle class, suburban, soccer mom church into a place where people with Harley-Davidson motorcycles, big tattoos, and hairy backs hang out—who are we to argue with him? If he wants to fill our churches with stale-smelling skateboarders, rap-reciting gang wannabes, or over-hyper computer nerds, what kind of objection can we possibly offer?

TRUTH FROM THE TRENCHES

People from rough-and-tumble backgrounds bring with them all their bad habits, poor decision-making abilities, damaged souls, and twisted thinking.

An influx of unruly new students might mean rethinking the budget to provide more resources for teens who have been more tempted to take money out of the offering plate than put it in. It may mean adding vehicles, rethinking space allocations, and recruiting more staff to help keep a lid on things. It may make interfacing your youth group with other church youth groups harder.

I learned that many other youth groups didn't really want to mix with the kids I was working with. There were a number of my kids who cheated at games, wouldn't hesitate to start a brawl, and had severe potty mouth.

For some reason, we attracted more than our share of young boys who were certified alpha males.

At one point I showed up at a camp with so many of these testosterone-filled young lads that I had to invent physically strenuous and challenging extracurricular activities just to take the edge off them so they could coexist with the guys from other churches. Doing that was a lot of work. There were days when I longed for a nice, docile, cooperative, respectful little youth group instead of the criminal types God had stuck me with.

They changed me, and they changed the church—and a number of them were changed in the process as well.

In nearly every conceivable way, reaching out to unchurched young people has repercussions for the church—and these can lead to uncomfortable change. But as C.S. Lewis observed, Christianity is designed to be comforting, not necessarily comfortable.

THE COMMAND

Outreach isn't really an option. We have marching orders, and we dare not take them lightly. The words of Jesus in Matthew 28 are pretty familiar to us all:

Then Jesus came to them and said, "All authority in heaven and on earth has been given to me. Therefore go and make disciples of all nations, baptizing them in the name of the Father and of the Son and of the Holy Spirit, and teaching them to obey everything I have commanded you. And surely I am with you always, to the very end of the age."

MATTHEW 28:18-20

With a little thought, a bit of experimentation, and the willingness to make changes, any church can begin to speak into the lives of teens who would otherwise never imagine themselves entering the orbit of a group of Christ-followers. But if the church sees itself as a fortress against the world and the unsavory characters who populate it; if it sees itself as surrounded by a moat of Christian-speak and a drawbridge of love that is lowered only to those who know the right passwords—the church will only (and without any hope for change) maintain the status quo. And doing so will be at the cost of excitement, adventure, struggle, joy, disappointment, and the privilege of seeing what God can do with a rough jewel once he gets it in his grip.

TRUTH FROM THE TRENCHES

Outreach isn't an option. We have marching orders, and we dare not take them lightly. The words of Jesus in Matthew 28 are pretty familiar to us all.

THE FUTURE: THEIRS AND OURS

The teens in a church's youth group are commonly referred to as the future of the church. What a church will become in the future has a great deal to do with whom we are populating it now. A few glances at the kids in many churches will tell you that we are destined for a very ingrown church, one populated and run by those who come from Christian homes only and have been raised in the church.

When those from the outside show up, they create a new dynamic for both the present and future. That new dynamic can work to quickly carry the church deeper into the community. It can communicate the core message of the gospel in a way that is relevant, understandable, and powerful—and one that can knock down a few walls of the Christian ghetto that so many have found themselves living in.

But it's not just the church that has a bright future by reaching kids at an early age. By reaching them early we save many from the pain, heartache, and struggles that their spiritually lost peers will experience as the natural course of living by their appetites and following what is wise in their own eyes. This benefit may not be realized while they're growing up, but they will look back at the arc of their lives and compare it to the trajectory of many of their peers who never came to Christ. And you may find yourself in possession of one of the most valuable things you can receive: a letter from a former teen thanking you for giving your life and your love to help them drink from the well of living water, Jesus.

How beautiful are the feet of those who bring good news!

ROMANS 10:15

ACTION PLAN

★ If it's true that the middle school/junior high age is where evangelism has a greater impact than most other stages of life, what would be some logical decisions and actions a church should make in this regard?

THINKING THROUGH REACHING THE UNCHURCHED

★ Knowing your church, what is your honest opinion on how the members would receive a bunch of teens who are obviously out of touch with the heart of Christ as they enter your doors, who bring messiness and numerous problems to the fellowship?

★ What might your church stand to gain, or lose, if it is able to reach significant numbers of unchurched teens?

★ What would you say are the sacred cows of your church community? How would members react if a few of those cows were slaughtered?

PART TWO

PUTTING IT TOGETHER

PUTTING TOGETHER THE KEY ELEMENTS BEFORE YOU LAUNCH

I am a glass-half-filled type of guy and not prone to pessimistic thinking. So please understand that I'm not exaggerating when I say that an effort to reach unchurched teens is ultimately doomed unless you have some key elements in place long before you launch. That's what the middle section of this book will be about. So here's one of those elements: doing effective outreach takes a point man or point woman, someone who not only has the heart to see the neediest of kids and teens come to Christ, but someone who actually has the skills, or ability, to connect with them and draw them in. You need both of those attributes to be strongly present in your point man or point woman.

THE RIGHT KIND OF POINT PERSON

Brady wanted to do a concert in order to reach the unsaved teens he saw everywhere. Brady has a huge heart, I mean huge. But he has next to zero skill in strategic thinking or attracting this type of teen. He put down big bucks for a band he thought would draw in street kids. They were a Christian band, of course, and his opening bands were also two Christian bands.

Not smart.

The results were predictable. The concert was pretty much an all-Christian event. (They gave an altar call anyhow, just to make sure.) Brady spent a ton of cash—most of which he didn't recoup—and ultimately had about zero net influence on the secular world his heart wanted to reach.

He did give the Christian kids a nice concert, though.

TRUTH FROM THE TRENCHES

Doing effective outreach takes a point man or point woman who not only has the heart to see the neediest of kids and teens come to Christ, but who also has the skills, or ability, to connect with them and draw them in.

Because Brady is a friend of mine, I weighed in early on his idea. "Are you sure you want to do this? I don't think that many secular kids know who this band is."

Brady insisted that the band he had chosen would draw them in like flies to a picnic. He is a little stubborn, and heck, it was his money—but still, I hated to see him both disappointed and broke. So I kept prodding and suggesting.

"Well, if I were you I would seed the opening acts with local secular bands who are likely to draw in their friends. They'll probably stay for the whole show."

"What?!" Brady said in near-amazement. "Non-Christian bands? They might swear or something."

I shrugged. "Well, if you want to reach the unsaved, you may have to make use of the good ol' unrighteous mammon."

"No other churches will support the concert if I do that!" Brady squealed. (Yes, he was squealing now.)

I shrugged again. "So?"

Brady went ahead with his plans and got the very outcome he didn't want. Everyone around him painted a happy face on the event and said things like "God prompted the people to come who he wanted to be there" . . . which is a nice, safe way to get around the fact that you missed your stated goals and that most likely your strategy and your plans were stinky.

Brady has the heart, but not the intuitive insight and street smarts, to navigate the world of secular teens. He makes a good second man, a great assistant, but not a good point man.

People with the heart and God-given ability to click with the secular world cannot be manufactured or produced via the educational system. These kinds of unique individuals have to be spotted and given the freedom and encouragement to go after non-Christian teens. They need to be allowed to create an environment where those kids will be welcomed and nurtured.

How? Well, the best way is to find that spiritual person with natural leadership abilities who always seems to have a lot of secular teens floating around him or her. This person could be a teacher or coach or nearly anyone who seems to enjoy students and who students seem to relate well to.

TRUTH FROM THE TRENCHES

People with the heart and God-given ability to click with the secular world cannot be manufactured or produced. These kinds of unique individuals have to be spotted and given the freedom and encouragement to go after non-Christian teens.

Many times these kinds of people are already doing ministry. Sometimes, they operate outside the walls of church ministry in parachurch groups such as Young Life or Campus Life—organizations that often attract those who may not be as drawn to the local church youth group.

FINDING A POINT PERSON

But recruiting some of these individuals may not be that easy. You may find an initial resistance to becoming part of the mission of an established church from people with the skill and talent to connect with secular youth.

Many of them are used to the kind of freedom and teamwork that comes with many parachurch outfits. They may see signing on with a church as entering a labyrinth-like operating system with various restrictions, even what they perceive (rightly or wrongly) as petty ones. Making such a choice could, at least at first, feel like wearing an anchor.

Those who run highly intuitive and aggressive outreach ministries are often suspicious of getting tangled up with the committees, boards, and politics in many local churches. Many know that local churches have a poor track record of appealing to and integrating those who come from the secular world.

There are more factors to enter into the mix.

Some churches go looking for someone "relevant to teens" among college-age individuals. While college-age people or young adults are often good candidates, please note that a college education is not necessary for this kind of person to be effective—and a seminary education often can even be counterproductive.

More than that, there's the myth that a person needs to be young to connect with students.

An effective outreach leader should not be measured so much on age or the cool factor as by his or her ability to communicate genuine love and interest, along with a natural sense of what works and what doesn't. Naturally, younger leaders usually have more energy and stamina than folks who are a little older—but there's a huge difference between working harder and working smarter. Often, older folks do this kind of ministry smarter than their younger counterparts.

The younger the point person, the more likely you will have to help guide them, apologize for them, and perhaps even protect them from those who want their hide. (Those rotten kids got into the pies that were supposed to be for the women's fellowship meeting the next day! The older youth worker, relying on past experiences, would have checked out the contents of the kitchen in advance—and hidden those pies.)

I've found that you can't always predict who the point person might be, so the man or woman who has a natural gift for connecting with kids outside the church might surprise you. Some will be diamonds in the rough that you'll have to work with patiently to encourage their gifts and build their skills— without evaporating their enthusiasm.

TRUTH FROM THE TRENCHES

Some point people will be diamonds in the rough that you'll have to work with patiently to encourage their gifts and build their skills—without evaporating their enthusiasm.

ONE SUCH DIAMOND

Jenny was one of our rough diamonds. She was one of our most effective leaders in grabbing teens from the fringes. She was energetic, warm, caring, and capable. New kids flooded into the youth ministry because of her efforts, love, and skill.

She was also young and somewhat careless.

She drove a small, beat-up car. She would pack it so full of kids that it looked like a circus car. The tires were bald, and we found out that she had no insurance. That pretty much panicked the more responsible guys on the leadership team because they knew that if she got into an accident hauling kids around with our blessings but with no insurance, we might have lawyers parked on our steps.

We insisted that she obtain insurance and offered to help by giving her a church minivan (which we insured) to drive. We also gave her some lectures about being responsible for the care of the students in her vehicle and how unappreciative parents are to get a phone call from the hospital.

She packed the minivan with teens and managed to ding it up nicely by backing into poles and clipping mailboxes, mostly because she was gabbing with the kids and not paying attention. (Ironically, she was a decent driver on the open road.) We'd grit our teeth, force a smile, and figure that these dings were the price we had to pay for Jenny to do her magic. We also gave her a lot of kidding about her demolition derby driving style.

Jenny was a valuable asset with a few liabilities that came with the total package. We chose to polish the asset and be patient with the liabilities while helping her change.

Regardless of how much a church may want to attract unreached teens, launching out after secular kids is generally premature unless there is a point person such as Jenny. On rare occasions I've seen teens themselves actually ignite and become proactive and effective in outreach to non-Christian friends, but those are aberrations—though welcome and wonderful ones—and not something you can create, program, or predict.

If there is no one who comes to mind who has the heart, skill, and immediate willingness to jump into this area, then now is a time to pray, watch, and prepare for the person that God will bring your way.

ACTION PLAN

★ When you think of the type of person who has the natural gift of connecting with teens inside and especially outside of the church, what name or names come to mind?

PUTTING IT TOGETHER: A CHURCH THAT *REALLY* WANTS TO REACH TEENS

I came onto the church campus this morning to find the parking lot, foyer, halls, and rooms littered with tiny, neon green Airsoft pellets. Obviously, the high schoolers had some fun last night.

This morning is the women's Bible study.

No doubt, there were far more pellets on the ground last night, but finding them all in the dark is next to impossible. Fortunately, the ladies who host the Bible study didn't seem too bothered by the odd litter. They're probably used to it by now.

A little kid came up to me with a paper cup full of pellets. I told him they were radioactive particles from a war with aliens that took place last night and if he could collect them all he would be doing the world a favor, and I would give him a dollar for every full cup he brought to me. Saving the world and getting paid for it seemed to appeal to him, so off he scampered to pick up pellets.

No one will get called on the carpet for the pellet residue. The janitor will not quit in frustration as the plastic bullets ricochet in his vacuum. Working with a group of people who really want to reach young people—and are willing to endure some of the nuisances that come with doing so—is really wonderful.

IS YOUR CHURCH READY?

In reality, even before you've found your point person who has both the heart and skill needed for the job, you'll need to make sure that your community of faith is truly ready and willing to take on the cost of going after the teens who are on the fringe. This is a bit trickier than it might appear. After all, if you ask people in your church if they want to reach the lost, they all have a knee-jerk reaction, one that forces them to say, "Why yes, of course!"

But there are always a number who don't really mean it.

What this statement means for many, of course, is "We want to reach the lost as long as they come in without a lot of problems for us to deal with, will start reading the Bible, volunteer in the nursery, bring extra food to the potluck, give up smoking and cussing right away, and basically act the way we want them to act."

In reality, few are likely to offer a homeless person a place on their couch or go looking for a hooker to invite to their women's Bible study. The price for this kind of thing is more than many can actually bear.

Too many want to reach the masses without having to actually embrace them.

OK, OK. It's easy to get cynical, but it is also too often this way. I'm right about this way more than I actually want to be.

I'm reminded of a story about Francis of Assisi, who was walking along a country road with his friends and fellow disciples when they heard the tinkling of a begging leper's bell warning travelers that he was approaching. Francis and his entourage edged toward the side of the road to give wide passage to this unfortunate creature with a feared and hideous disease.

Watching the man in his rotting clothes and rotting flesh stumble down the road, Francis came to the realization that the man's wretched condition might get him sympathy and pity from afar, but he would never get what he longed for most: human touch.

To the astonishment of his friends as well as to the leprous man, Francis stepped into the middle of the road and, with open arms, advanced toward him.

The leper fearfully worked his little bell to warn off this madman, but Francis, ignoring it, wrapped the crumbling, disgusting beggar in a huge bear hug, whispered the blessings of God to him, and then crowned his actions with a kiss on the poor man's face.

That kind of thing is why we remember Francis today and why he was so effective—he was not content to love at a distance.

And that kind of mind-set must typify any church that wants to reach those outside its walls. You never know who God will choose to put in your path.

TRUTH FROM THE TRENCHES

Loving up close, where it's dangerous, and not from a distance: that's the kind of mind-set that must typify any church that wants to reach those outside its walls.

A CHURCH THAT'S WILLING TO PAY THE PRICE

Because I have a long history of doing this sort of thing, I'm often asked to consult with churches that are considering doing actual outreach. After about fifteen minutes of discussion, most of them abandon the idea.

I recall sitting with a lovely group of committee people who were wisely trying to weigh the cost of outreach. We gathered in a large and historic fellowship hall; the cookies were homemade and tasted marvelous. I munched on them as they proudly described the heritage of the hall.

"Is this the largest room you have?" I inquired.

"Yes. This is where we would have our outreach activities for the teens," they answered politely.

I got up and walked over to one of the windows.

"Well, if you end up achieving what we're talking about, you can expect to have two or three window panes like these broken by flying balls, broom handles, careless horseplay, or some poor kid's head."

They nearly choked on their cookies.

I wandered around the large hall pointing out the future of the room. "You can assume there will be some interesting-looking gouges on this nice hardwood floor, and a few bad words written on this desktop. Any of the furniture in here will be jumped on, drenched and discolored with soda, and full of crumbs. I should also point out that you'll sometimes find that all the toilet paper has disappeared from the bathroom after an event—and by the way, this is *with* supervision."

I gazed at some horror-filled expressions. Their reaction was as if I was describing a fourth horseman of the apocalypse.

So I took the time, and in great detail, to explain the parasitical nature of this kind of teen (and actually, of most teens in general). I gave them a ballpark idea of the cost not only to their facilities but also to their budget. I carefully worked to help them understand that these things might even affect church attendance for a while, particularly on Sunday mornings.

They quickly thanked me for my insight and voted to table the idea until a later meeting—which is typical church-speak for "We ain't gonna do this crazy thing!" You see, they valued preserving their historic building more than they did reaching out to unbelieving teens. They would have loved to do both, but forced to make a choice, they did. And they made the wrong one.

Sometimes the cost to a church is dissatisfied and disgruntled members.

A family with teenagers recently left our church. Their explanation was that the youth group was "too dangerous for our kids." Both parents had come to faith as adults and were doing their best to raise their kids in a distinctly Christian environment. When the kids were young, they loved Sunday school. As preteens they were starting to take music lessons so they could play the worship songs that they heard all day long. Eventually, they became teenagers and moved into the middle school department, where a high priority is placed on dragging in youth for whom Christianity, unless otherwise revealed to them, is a mystery.

The parents realized that their kids were now surrounded by the very kind of teens they had worked hard to keep their children from. The most horrifying thing about it was the fact that these immersions took place at the church's youth group. The danger of a bad infection from the secular kids outweighed the possibility of a good infection leaking out from their kids. So they left.

As you know, there are few churches that celebrate when core, committed families leave the fellowship.

TRUTH FROM THE TRENCHES

Sometimes the cost to a church that really goes after the unchurched is dissatisfied and disgruntled members.

Consider the cost that your success will bring in other ways. For instance, you may need to rethink your budget. You may need to rethink the use of your facilities. (The hordes of new middle school kids prompted one church I worked with to get rid of pews in favor of those movable stacking chairs so that we could have more room. That decision sparked the infamous Pew Wars.) You may need to find more helpers and staff. You may need to rethink how you will spend your time. (Be sure to include the hours required to vacuum up the hundreds of Airsoft pellets scattered around the campus!)

A CHURCH THAT'S WILLING TO LOOSEN UP (AND PAY THE PRICE FOR IT)

Be honest. Do you get bugged if someone lights up a cigarette in the church parking lot? How would you react if you knew that a couple of kids showed up to a meeting stoned, or if you found out they'd smuggled a joint into camp? What if the girls you've been working with for so long to connect with the gospel came to a pool party wearing swimsuits that were barely there? Suppose the f-bomb came hurtling across the church hallway? What if there were some terribly rank rap songs leaking out of the ear buds attached to some of the iPods?

Even if you can handle those situations with grace and appropriateness, can your church?

Some churches make a big deal out of things that are not a big deal to the teens outside of Christian circles. Some refuse to allow any music to be played on a road trip or in the youth room other than Christian music. Some expect a standard for church activities that is baffling for secular kids. I do believe that youth groups should have clear and reasonable standards for those who want to participate. Drug use and drinking are absolutely not allowed, filthy language is frowned on, girls and guys can't share sleeping quarters on overnighters, and public displays of affection aren't appropriate. The key to these kinds of rules is that they're sensible to almost all teens, Christian or not, and generally supported by the community, the schools, and most families. Secular kids don't usually rebel at clear, sensible, and logical standards that are in force in church meetings and in homes, schools, and sports programs.

Few of the things that Christians get so high and holy about are clear biblical mandates. Many times a silly legalism sets in—such as declaring all R-rated movies off limits when many PG-13 rated movies are far more foul and offensive to a Christian's morals. (Research movies carefully first at sites like www.screenit.com; just two examples of movies that you'd never get to take a teen to see if you flatly declared all R-rated movies off limits are *The Passion of the Christ* and *Saving Private Ryan*. Meanwhile, some PG-13 movies are filled with junk.)

My personal favorite whipping boy of many churches is the celebration of Halloween, a holiday for which I'll provide a whole lot of ammo on how to use in a positive way later in this book. For a long time Christians had no particular gripe with Halloween, but for the last couple of decades many churches have come to the conclusion that the holiday enjoyed by so many vampire wannabes is the epitome of evil in our world.

Never mind that the rest of the world is out in wild costumes grabbing up candy from their neighbors. A lot of Christians migrate to church basements, where they can stay away from evil by dressing up as a Bible character (except for Satan, Delilah, Judas, Jezebel, and presumably Rahab in her hooker days) and pass out candy to each other. The key is that there's no effort to associate with the world in a way that would honor Christ.

We think we're being holy by staying away from the obvious evil of bats, spider webs, ghosts, cute-looking witches, Darth Vaders, and vampires. The rest of the world thinks we're nutty for interpreting something so silly and benign as a thing so fearful that it's worth hiding from. When holiness looks a whole lot like nuttiness, you may have a problem.

Should we get on our high horse about the pagan roots of Halloween? Any knowledgeable unbeliever can knock us right off that horse by mentioning the pagan roots that are attached to Christmas, and questioning why our churches say nothing about Easter egg hunts or Valentine's Day.

A church that really wants to reach the unsaved may have to rethink its issues. Which issues are fundamental to biblical integrity and which are reactions to social situations? In some cases, a church may have to become dualistic in the sense of allowing for differing viewpoints: letting those in their congregation who are against Halloween be against it, and allowing those reaching out to youth the freedom to milk the holiday for all they can get.

Not everyone will be happy with the avenues that those reaching out to teens are choosing to venture down. Some will go on a tirade if you organize a paintball weekend or have Airsoft battles in the sanctuary. "The youth workers are encouraging violence!" they'll moan to anyone willing to listen. (By the way, I'll have more on Airsoft and how to use it to draw teens in chapter 10.)

Our middle school pastor wanted to attract more of the secular kids who had been coming to his midweek program to try out his Bible study class on Sunday. He decided to take the middle school crew out for a pizza lunch and then to the theater to see *The Simpsons Movie* (which had just released) after the Sunday morning Ignite Bible study (formerly called Sunday school).

A new family had come to our church in recent months. They had a middle schooler who wanted to get in on the action.

One of the parents blew a fuse. Didn't we know that *The Simpsons* were just plain evil? (Uh, no. The thought never dawned on us, actually.) Naturally, the parent forbade the teen from the day.

But that wasn't good enough. She also went on a rampage.

Finally, I explained to the parents that not only did the staff stand by the decision of our middle school pastor, most of the leadership team enjoyed *The Simpsons* and planned on either seeing the movie or buying the DVD when it was available.

The new family instantly left the church, amazed at our lack of spiritual discernment and wisdom.

A CHURCH FULL OF GRACE

Kids who come from a home where drugs or alcohol use are prevalent, where language is vulgar, and where morality is not practiced, bring those "family values" with them. These are the kids that many Christian parents fear most because they may pollute the clean waters that the parents have been so diligent to keep their kids swimming in.

A church full of grace understands the nature of the teens it is working with. While setting clear standards for expected behavior, a grace-full church will work with those teens in a caring and kind way.

You may be surprised at how often grace is called into play.

In my early twenties, I was hired as a middle school pastor. The church had eleven kids in that age group, but I knew where I could find a lot more. After a year, we had eleven church kids and about three hundred formerly unchurched kids coming to youth group—so many that I had to ask for the church bus to go to the bad part of town to pick them up.

The vehicle was a classic school bus painted blue with a large glass rear door under which some genius had painted "Follow me to Sunday school!" Our volunteer staff went out to grab the kids while I stayed on campus and made sure all my programming ducks were in a row.

Somewhere in the few miles between the bad part of town and the church campus, the guys in the back egged on a not-so-smart but well-endowed girl to pull up her blouse top and bra and press her exposed breasts against the rear window of the church bus.

"Follow me to Sunday school!" Now there is an advertisement!

The volunteer leaders on the bus were oblivious to what had been going on, but by the time they arrived at the campus the giggling kids had let the word out— and before the bus was unloaded I was waiting outside as the girl walked off.

"Let's you and I have a talk," I said sternly, but softly. By now, the girl was red-faced with embarrassment and tearfully repentant. She did not need to be scolded.

"I have to send you home today," I said. But I also knew her home situation, and I added, "But I won't say anything about this incident as long as you promise me that you won't do anything dumb again."

"Can I come back next week?" she pleaded through tears.

"Of course. We want you to come back. I won't say any more about this from here on out."

She thanked me, and I briefed a female staff person on the conversation. I told her to drive the young lady home. For the kids, it was a hilarious event that eventually died down as everyone moved on to the next scandal or act of stupidity. But eventually—you guessed it—what happened found its way into the ranks of the rest of the church.

Some were too shocked to say anything, some wanted to make sure that harsh punishment would be meted out to this tramp (a public stoning and lifetime banishment from the church grounds seemed to be what they were pushing for), but still others surprised me by the understanding and grace they offered as I explained what I knew about the girl and her home life. They also gave me their support for how I had handled the situation.

And some knew that they had made a mistake to hire me. After all, just look at the kind of riffraff showing up nowadays, they reasoned.

TRUTH FROM THE TRENCHES

A church full of grace understands the nature of the teens it is working with. While setting clear standards of expected behavior, a grace-full church will work with those teens in a caring and kind way.

A CHURCH AND YOUTH GROUP THAT WILL INTEGRATE EVEN PAGANS (OR, A YOUTH GROUP THAT ACTS LIKE CHRISTIANS)

One of the biggest hurdles to effective outreach to students can be the Christian teens in the youth group. (And, by extension, their parents.) Most youth groups have an established pecking order. A few highly energized girls lead many of them and quite a few youth groups have an unusual amount of teens in Christian schools or who are home schooled. New kids—especially tough, streetwise alpha males (which have always been my primary target group)— really mess with the established order.

Of course, where you have alpha males, you usually have some very attractive girls circling nearby. Attractive girls make other girls feel nervous and inferior. Attractive pagan girls don't have much use for Christian niceties either. (To be quite honest, Christian girls can be just as catty and cliquish as their non-Christian counterparts. Claws can come out fast.) The new kids are seen as interlopers invading the domain of the long-time church kids.

Resentment can grow. "Us and them" sentiment can flourish. The oil of the world and the water of the Christian community often do not mix well. You should expect some Christian kids to undermine the efforts to bring in new kids.

Part of the solution is to make sure to incorporate your students into the entire outreach strategy from the start. Encourage them to bring their unbelieving or unchurched friends. Challenging church kids to be spiritual leaders and discussing, in advance, the kinds of problems and dilemmas that can take place can help ease the process.

Because every youth group has different dynamics and its own unique chemistry, there is no magic bullet that can be used to slay the potential problems that come from flooding an established group with newcomers who think, behave, and respond very differently.

A CHURCH PREPARED TO WELCOME CHALLENGES AND CHANGES

Some churches have gone so far as to create what is effectively two youth groups: one primarily filled with Christian teens, and one dominated by newbies. (I'm not making this my hard-and-fast recommendation, but it is something that can be looked at.) Nothing will shut down an active outreach-oriented youth ministry quicker than having the parents of the church kids feeling as if their teens have not been ministered to, or have been marginalized in order to reach the unchurched.

Adults in the church need to understand what their role is if clusters of odd-acting (and maybe even odd-looking!) teens start to show up on the church campus from time to time. Besides supporting the outreach efforts, adults can be part of the solution by choosing to wander by a group of kids they don't know, welcome them, and express interest in them. Maybe parents in your ministry can sell concessions or help serve in some tangible way, allowing them to subtly integrate throughout the ministry.

In short, a church must be prepared to welcome the challenges and changes that effective outreach will bring.

In the late '60s, many people and staff members at most churches looked down on those young people who dove into the hippie culture. Here and there you could find a Christian leader who could get past the whiff of patchouli oil, beads, and long hair in order to love on these teens or young adults. Those isolated leaders found a deep hunger for God in these counter-cultural young people, and their churches began to be filled with them.

One Southern California church found itself in this position, and many in the church were none too happy about it. The subject of the church being taken over by dirty hippies became the focal point of one particularly raucous board meeting. The complaint was not stated as such but was put in a more palatable manner—the actual voiced concern was with the number of young people who were attending church barefoot.

"Why is this a problem?" asked the pastor, who knew full well what the real issue was.

"It's the carpet," fumbled one of the board members. "The oil and dirt from their feet will ruin the carpet."

"So that's it? If it were not for the carpet, you would be fine with these young people attending service even if they were barefoot?" the pastor asked.

The board nodded in agreement and the meeting closed.

Later that night the pastor went into the church and single-handedly ripped out all the carpet.

With their excuse gone, a number of board members steamed away from the church in anger. And that church went on to become one of the larger ministries in the area, with many of those dirty hippie kids eventually taking the mantle of Christian leadership.

The pastor wisely opted to allow the church to become the church Jesus wanted it to be instead of the church some in the congregation wanted it to be.

By the way, the person who told me this story was one of the board members who left in anger and disgust. Years later, he humbly saw that God had a plan bigger than his prejudice.

ACTION PLAN

★ What would it cost your church to focus on reaching out to the unchurched teens in your area?

PUTTING IT TOGETHER: EMBRACE THE PROCESS

keep seeing them show up on Facebook: pictures of former members of youth groups I've led. Except now they're adults. But they're still into posting what they used to look like.

As I see the young faces, lithe bodies, and dated hairstyles, I reflect on the trajectories of those lives. Some blossomed quickly; they could have been poster children for what it should look like when one goes from ragged unbeliever to Christ-follower. Others have had a Christian life of stumbles, inconsistencies, and ups and downs, yet they're still hanging in there. Some vanished from the faith, only to resurface years later, battered and bruised, but now with a much deeper commitment to the Lord. And some are still out there in deep orbit, a long ways from the safety of Christ.

NOT QUITE EASY AND PAIN-FREE

One of the hardest concepts to communicate to people is that maturing as a Christian is a process. Big time. With a capital P.

Most of us would like to think that the conversion of souls is instantaneous, pain-free, and positively altering for a lifetime. And then there is the way it really is. Sometimes it takes a long, long time before anything that resembles fruit emerges from a person's life. There are a number of reasons for this.

For a believing young person the spiritual transformation is mixed with the physical, emotional, and social transformations that are also taking place as they mature. And *those* maturity processes are loaded with all kinds of wild swings. Teens and young adults are often driven by impulses unchecked by mature thinking. (Heck, this is true for plenty of adults and even older adults too!)

A student who has solid, involved Christian parenting has a team backing him or her to help them avoid acting on some mood they might be having to avoid church or the youth group or even other Christians altogether. The parents can remind them of Christ's standards, principles and values that many teenagers will not choose if they are on their own.

But for the teenager from an unchurched environment there may not be any kind of fail-safe system to keep them spiritually connected when mood swings, social pressures, or other factors line up at their door and knock loudly, shouting at them to walk away from Christian community. The potential for these teens to slip away from the faith is much higher than for those from Christ-centered homes.

Also, there is an expectation on the part of many folks in the church that once the savages have come to Christ they now should be tamed, clothed, and ready to sing in the choir.

This is a false expectation.

TRUTH FROM THE TRENCHES

We would like to think that the conversion of souls is instantaneous, pain-free, and positively altering for a lifetime. And then there is reality. Sometimes it takes a long, long time before anything that resembles fruit emerges from a person's life.

In fact, for a while there may not be a great deal of obvious, on-the-surface difference between the pre-Christian and now-Christian teen. That's because the process of the Holy Spirit guiding a life is one that typically moves slowly— sanding, chipping, and shaping instead of exploding and rebuilding.

I still recall, with a chuckle, how one young new believer excitedly told me that "knowing Christ is the best _____ (insert a very significant cuss word here) thing I have every experienced!"

It was a genuine testimony, sincere, honest, without guile . . . and completely unrepeatable.

God was working on this young believer but the young man apparently had not yet converted his choice of adjectives.

In many years of working with teens from tough backgrounds or deeply secular homes, I've seen kids who thought they were doing well spiritually because they only smoked pot once a week instead of daily (and I think they actually *were* doing well, all things considered). I have met kids whose parents worked hard to pull them away from the Christian faith, declaring to their friends and family that their children were involved in a cult and that yours truly was a cult leader on a par with Manson, Koresh, or Jones—minus the Kool-Aid, of course.

MIGHT AS WELL ENJOY THE RIDE

The process of having our lives changed is a long-term deal. God is still converting parts of me that I never realized or wanted to realize needed conversion. And God will have his hands full as he begins to re-craft the lives of some of the teens I know and work with.

Things can turn interesting very quickly.

In a congregation I once served in, I had a high school student whose mother was very supportive of the positive changes going on with her son.

She actually wanted to join him at worship on Sunday mornings, but couldn't, because of her work schedule. But her partner, who also had been impressed by the newfound joy in the young man, had already started to show up at worship. Oh, did I say that her partner was a woman? And that it became an uncertainty, for some, regarding the best approach to this woman?

Dealing with unchurched teens can be a tough game . . . and now the whole church gets to play. (Exercise: Ask yourself how your community of faith would react to the real life situation just described. Is it prepared to handle people, such as these women, with love and grace? Does it know how to genuinely embrace the sinner without compromising biblical values and standards? And by the way: how would *you* react?)

There may be a need to engage proactively with those whose expectations for new converts are too unrealistic. Explain the wild baggage, wacky home situations, and rudderless parenting that, for many teams, often come with the package. The key thing is to soften the expectation among church members who are looking for instantaneous and unwavering conversion out of every student.

Oh—and enjoy the ride as you watch God work in the lives of these tough cases. You just may find your spiritual growth taking off in new directions along with them.

TRUTH FROM THE TRENCHES

Dealing with unchurched teens can be a tough game . . . and now the whole church gets to play.

ACTION PLAN

★ Think of the most recent situation in your youth group or church that required extra grace without compromising biblical convictions. Did you, or are you, responding in this way? If not, what can be different so you can respond this way?

PUTTING IT TOGETHER: THE POINT PERSON, THE PEOPLE, THE PROCESS

★ Would your church be willing to take a dualistic stance on sometimes-touchy programs, issues, or holidays, including paintball, Airsoft wars, or Halloween events?

★ How would your youth group react if a whole crew of unchurched teens started showing up?

★ What are some situations in which your church, your leadership team, or your youth group may need to display plenty of grace?

★ What situations need a firm hand? What situations need both a firm hand *and* grace?

PART THREE

MAKING IT WORK

MAKING IT WORK: LAUNCH TIME

Now, assuming you have a willing and able point person and assuming that your church is excited about the possibility of flooding the premises with teens from the fringes and is ready to support these endeavors, the logical question becomes: how do you do this thing?

From the start, we need to understand that there is no program or magic formula that's guaranteed to produce the results you're hoping for. There are general principles that tend to work, and I will offer a whole bunch of ideas that may get you started. But different regions of different countries have different tilts on things, and every culture has a rhythm that works for it (and many that don't). So having a solid understanding of the potential pitfalls and minefields that come with the kinds of teens you're working with is vital.

You'll also need to view outreach activity as experimental in nature. Sometimes you will hit on an idea or activity that really works and is almost timeless, other times that the idea works one year and bombs the next, and still other times when the idea goes directly into the tank.

Keep in mind that the thoughts and suggestions provided in this book are not designed to be templates but instead yanks on the light cord of your imagination. You may think many of my suggestions are unworkable—and that would be OK—but they may spark ideas for something that will work for your group.

This is exactly what I'm hoping for.

The rest of this chapter is filled with a number of key ideas, big picture stuff, to get you started.

TRUTH FROM THE TRENCHES

In youth ministry, outreach activities are often experimental in nature. There are times you'll hit on an idea or activity that really works and is almost timeless, other times that the idea works one year and bombs the next, and still other times when the idea goes directly into the tank.

AIM AT THE GUYS

There's a timeless principle of youth ministry that says, "If you want growth, aim your energy and activity at males and then you'll get females as well. Aim primarily at girls, and that is pretty much all you will get." What motivates guys is different from what motivates girls. Guys are attracted by sports, challenges, and different kinds of activities—in short, the hobbies of many teen boys.

The hobby of most girls is guys; if you don't believe it, just be a fly on the wall and listen in on some teen conversations. You'll find that guys, when they do get around to talking, primarily talk about one kind of thing and relationship-focused girls talk about another.

The gist of their dialogue should be enough to convince you of the truism of the "aim at guys" principle.

The typical youth group is often driven and controlled by the girls. This is fine if the objective is a female group, but problematic if you're looking to do coed outreach. This doesn't mean that we abandon the girls—at all—but it does mean that when we are creating a coed activity, we should do our best to consider if it will interest alpha males. Girls-only activities are both effective and to be encouraged, but we need to make our outreach focus for whole-group ministry tilted to those things that guys will buy into with ease. (There is, of course, a caveat to all this: a bunch of attractive young girls will always attract guys—but for all the wrong reasons. The potential problems that come along with such an outreach "strategy" are often not worth the hassle.)

Another factor in this principle is that many guys have been groomed to become leaders. A youth group dominated by strong female leaders is a quick turnoff to most guys. So key leadership must strongly be male in order to attract guys from the outside. At the same time, I applaud and am heartened by the number of women who are in the trenches in full-time youth ministry; God can certainly use take-charge-and-get-it-done females. (Look at Deborah in the book of Judges.) But the truth is that alpha males will look to other males to lead them.

KNOW WHERE YOU'RE TAKING THEM

An effective outreach program without some solid thinking about what you will do to engage, enfold, and disciple new believers is kind of like a woman who gives birth and then abandons the baby in the hospital.

Keep in mind that most teens from unchurched backgrounds have virtually nothing that motivates them to be part of a church—outside of their own interest and desire. Parents may be mildly supportive, apathetic, or even hostile to their child spending time attending church or reading the Bible.

In my experience, a young person who comes to faith will often be instrumental in leading parents and siblings to Christ. But I've also seen some parents react fearfully or suggest that their teen has gotten involved in a cult. Keeping strong and consistent communication with the parents of teens from unchurched homes will help negate most big problems. (See Making It Work Through Family Outreach near the end of this book.)

TRUTH FROM THE TRENCHES

The key to helping unchurched teens who come into your fellowship with very little or no support from their parents is keeping strong, consistent communication. This will help negate most big problems.

While much of your spiritual growth plan will have to be dependent on the age, background, and maturity of the teens you reach, there are some logical steps to develop in harmony with outreach activities. For instance, if we're connecting with teens outside of the church family, how do we begin the process of helping them feel welcomed by our community of faith? Do we bring them in only once they have professed faith, or do we invite them to check us out and participate even if they've not yet declared themselves a believer? What we decide often has implications.

- ★ Do we embrace the idea of allowing teens to belong before they believe?
- ★ Do we slap the Communion elements out of the hand of an unbeliever who innocently takes them?
- ★ Do we lower expectations and standards for those who join us without allegiance to our Master?

★ Is it wise or even realistic to plunge a new believer into things that require a measure of growth and understanding?

★ If we have a brand new believer, just where is the best place for them to start their journey with our spiritual family?

We need to think in advance about the entry points and the environment needed to encourage growth in new believers. We may also need to protect them from the unfriendly (or even weird) elements and people we have running around our church family and from things like mind-numbing meetings that do very little to help someone new in their faith.

Among the tips that can help with this process is to make sure that we have a thought-out follow-up strategy in place. What will be the next step for a teen who has made a commitment to Christ?

★ If the next step is to become more familiar with the Bible, we probably shouldn't hand over a big, thick King James Version. A simple New Testament or gospels portion in a modern language version would far better meet the needs.

★ If one of the next steps is to join other believers in an age-appropriate small group or to become part of a Bible study, we may need to make sure our new teen feels comfortable even though his or her level of understanding is minimal. This may mean things like not putting them on the spot to read passages or answer questions, and probably not thrusting them into a group of long-time disciples who are studying the minor prophets in great depth.

★ If one of the next steps is developing connections in the Christian community, we can work with some of our mature Christian teens to be prepared to take these new ones under their wings.

The key here is not to assume that growth and assimilation will take place, but to create a soil in which this newly erupting seed can sprout best.

TRUTH FROM THE TRENCHES

The key for a new believer is not to assume that growth and assimilation will take place, but to create a soil in which this newly erupting seed can sprout best.

MIDDLE SCHOOL IS EASIER THAN HIGH SCHOOL

When you want to do outreach, middle school is the easier age group to draw in. Middle school kids are the lepers of the teenage years. Most people ignore them. High schoolers dismiss them. Youth pastors routinely assign some underling to work with them.

Awkward, immature, hyper, at times stupid, mischievous—and yet wondrously innocent and open in many ways to new possibilities—this age group has a few key elements that a smart youth worker can capitalize on.

They travel in groups

More than high schoolers, middle school kids travel (and behave) as pack animals. Get one, you get them all. Middle schoolers are as relational as you can get.

Few adults like them

Middle schoolers go nuts when an adult (other than one of their parents) considers them important. Be nice to a middle school kid and he or she will be your friend for life—or at least a month. (Remember, they have short attention spans.)

They're not mobile

Middle schoolers can't get around very well. Anyone who will haul them somewhere is a buddy. You can fill a van for a youth event any day of the week by telling one middle schooler that you'll pick up him or her and any of their friends after school. You'll get half the school if you mention you'll be stopping for ice cream on the way.

They're anxious for fun

Middle schoolers want to have a good time. They want to get out of the house. They usually don't have jobs or a lot of serious homework, but they do have a lot of free time. Do something fun and the word gets out.

They're open spiritually

Middle schoolers still have tender hearts. Cynical thinking and heavy temptations have not yet polluted many of them. If you can maneuver around the short attention spans, you'll find middle school teens drink in concepts about God like water.

Abstract thinking is within reach

Children have a hard time with abstract thinking—and much of the Christian faith requires abstract thinking. For middle schoolers, being able to think in abstract ways is refreshing; it's like having their eyes opened for the first time as they grasp big picture ideas.

They have little baggage

Relatively few middle schoolers carry around the kind of negative baggage that they will accumulate years later. Their hearts are freer, and they can often be directed down paths that will keep them that way.

TRUTH FROM THE TRENCHES

If you can maneuver around the short attention spans, you'll find middle school teens drink in concepts about God like water.

While only a special kind of person will immerse himself or herself into the world of middle school, this age group is a terrific place to start an outreach ministry. With a bit of thought and work, a large number of these teens will move on toward maturity and service as high school students.

EXPLOIT YOUR OBVIOUS STRENGTHS

Imagine a church full of skateboarders. No, really, imagine what it would be like to have stale-smelling teens with wheels under their feet infesting every available inch of concrete around your church. Imagine wax and missing concrete chips on the planter boxes from grinds, or handrails to the sanctuary being used for rail slides. Imagine a couple dozen skateboards stacked in the hall before a meeting. Imagine the, uh, interesting imagery of skater T-shirt art clothing the bodies of dozens of kids.

The leader of this pack could be you. Isn't that a great thought?

It certainly was me in my greenhorn start as a middle school youth pastor. Because I was a skater and surfer, and I understood as well as participated in that culture, connecting with those teens was easy for me. I never really intended for the youth group to become overrun with one element—it just happened. Perhaps it was a God thing, I don't know. After all, nobody else seemed able to connect with those kids.

Everyone has something they do or are involved in that a particular group of teens might find fascinating. These strengths are the natural connection points for us to use in reaching those outside the church.

★ It could be hunting, fishing, or scrapbooking.
★ It could be a sport of some kind.
★ It could be mechanics, music, or gaming.
★ It could be something considered nerdy by jocks but really cool by nerds.

Pursuing your natural connection points may mean that you end up with a youth group where the majority carry Buck knives, have greasy hands, and smell of gasoline—or where they all look like Bill Gates clones.

The point is, the most natural place to start is right where you are. If God decides to use you to change the complexion of the youth group by flooding it with Goth kids, snowboarders, computer geeks, or wrestlers, that's his business.

Thinking about what you do and inviting a teen who has a similar interest to join you—and to bring a friend along as well—takes very little effort. The easiest and most genuine kind of outreach is sharing who God made you to be with teens who are made the same way.

I've become just about every sort of servant there is in my attempts to lead those I meet into a God-saved life. I did all this because of the Message. I didn't just want to talk about it; I wanted to be in on it!

I CORINTHIANS 9:22, 23, THE MESSAGE

BIG VS. SMALL

Most of us like to think in terms of numbers and volumes, and the more teens we can get to with the good news, the better. Fill the hall, pack the stadium: this becomes our thinking. But small often can be the much more desirable option.

Pulling off some of the big ideas that might be in your imagination, or even in this book, requires a staff and a budget, but other things can be done with little money and in a small, personal, and meaningful manner. A carful of kids may be better than a vanful—and much easier to get to know. Having a half-dozen kids over for a barbecue and a night of gaming often can be more productive in kingdom time than a big extravaganza.

Some people are built to handle groups, and some are built only to handle individuals. Figuring out your personality and gifting in this area is helpful as you craft your outreach efforts.

The key reason small is often so powerful is that "we" don't come to Christ— "I" do. Entrance to the kingdom is not a group affair, but an individual one.

A number of the ideas and much of the drift in this book are toward more organized and larger outreach efforts, but these are only some of the possible ways of reaching teens. You may find God guiding you toward a much leaner but equally important way to connect with young people who need Christ.

TRUTH FROM THE TRENCHES

Some people are built to handle groups, and some are built only to handle individuals. Figuring out your personality and gifting in this area is helpful as you craft your outreach efforts.

MENTOR OUTREACH

One highly effective way for outreach to take place on a smaller level is mentoring. Mentoring is connecting with one or two kids in some area of shared interest and building a relationship with them through genuine friendship. For example, if you're a gifted seamstress, teaching a couple of teens how to sew provides great opportunities to get to know those students. Once teens know you and like you, they'll give you permission to speak into their lives.

ACTION PLAN

★   How will you know which activities, Bible studies, or events will ring as strongly—or even more strongly—with males as females? What are some examples of those activities—and how do you make them still attractive for girls?

MAKING IT WORK THROUGH POSITIVE CHRISTIAN CONTACT

There is often a natural order of things when it comes to reaching secular, or unchurched, teens. Many secular teens are often very suspicious of "religion." They have the idea that the church is trying to take advantage of them ("all the church wants is your money") or that the church wants to make everyone into a ranting Jesus freak and put them on street corners to preach. "Religion" (which is how secular teenagers see what we call our faith) is something for kooks and emotional cripples, not for the healthy, robust teen, especially the male one.

The first step in building a relationship with secular kids is often through something we can call positive Christian contact. This can be anything that connects the Christian world with the secular world in a positive way.

Usually, this kind of event or activity has no direct Christian message, although it may start in prayer, involve blessing a meal, and have ethical guidelines that everyone is expected to follow (watch your language, no drinking or drugs, those sorts of things). A few examples might be a day of playing paintball, a trip to the beach or to go water skiing, a skateboard safari, a game night, or anything else that draws in teens who are looking for something fun to do.

The main point of those activities is simply to create an environment that's fun, attractive, and compelling for your youth group members to invite their secular friends to check out.

TRUTH FROM THE TRENCHES

The main point of positive Christian contact is simply to create an environment that's fun, attractive, and compelling for your youth group members to invite their secular friends to check out.

I understand some people will be frustrated if they collect a whole slew of unbelievers for an activity and then not have a chance to hammer those kids with the gospel. For some groups, a commercial break for God is almost mandatory at each and every activity.

Be very, very careful about this kind of thinking. There is no biblical mandate that forces us to verbally present the gospel just because we've gathered teens together. In some of these situations we're much more effective if we present the message by interest, love, and genuine caring directed toward the students—and, of course, being ready to share about the hope that resides within when we have the proper opening. But a poorly timed or high-pressure presentation will actually work against us as it's awkward for all and even embarrassing for the Christian teens who brought their friends.

IMPORTANT STUFF FOR POSITIVE CHRISTIAN CONTACT EVENTS

Here are a few strategic issues that you shouldn't neglect.

Collect names and contact information

Seek to get names and contact information from every new teen that comes. Depending on the venue you use, you can do different things to encourage getting names—holding a prize drawing is one such idea.

Send brief thank you cards

Make sure to send each new student a thank you card within a week after your event. Most teens rarely get personal mail, so a handwritten note sends a powerful and positive message. But it's important to also remember this: keep the card brief and don't get too aggressive on these first contact opportunities. When an adult starts calling or even inviting adolescents to participate on a deeper level, the situation is often viewed with skepticism—maybe even seen as creepy—by secular parents who are worried about predators.

Have another event on the horizon

Make sure to have another event or activity in mind that would be of interest to these same teens. Presuming the students have a good time, they'll probably be willing, and hopefully excited, to attend another activity if they're aware of it. Have the promotional information for the next activity ready to hand out as teens leave the event.

Watch for the natural leaders

Keep an eye out for the teens who seem to have persuasion ability with their peers; they are the natural leaders, the charismatic characters. These are the teens you'll want to know and win if they come back. They're the ones who can influence the growth you're aiming for or, if they have a negative experience, turn their peers away.

IT DOESN'T HAVE TO BE THE SUPER BOWL OF OUTREACH

Keep in mind that positive Christian contact does not have to be a big, massive, crazy event. It can be very small and niche-oriented: a handful of guys playing video games; a group of girls having a sleepover; a small crew of people using the church sound system to have band practice.

The nature of the activity used to make connections should tell you where and when a gospel presentation or Bible study is appropriate. Overnight activities such as a camping trip often offer an ideal setting around a fire to engage in authentic sharing of what knowing Christ is about. On the other hand, trying to wedge in a presentation in the middle of an amusement park outing is usually futile, not to mention frustrating, for all involved.

The teens who have the ability to bring other students to your ministry are the ones who are sensitive to the quality and appropriateness of what you're doing. If your activities are dull or boring, or if they feel that presenting an opportunity to make a commitment to Christ is coming off like a high-pressure sales pitch, you may be choking your gold-laying geese. Those teens who have natural sensitivities and are bringing other students out are great sounding boards for when and how to deliver such messages.

TRUTH FROM THE TRENCHES

Positive Christian contact does not have to be a big, massive, crazy event. It can be very small, even niche-oriented, and still be quite successful.

ACTION PLAN

★ How have you used simple events as positive Christian contact?
   What activities would work in your ministry in the future?

MAKING IT WORK THROUGH SEASONS, TIMING, AND RUNWAYS

8

It was supposed to be the big evangelistic event of the year. The band was popular and the venue location fun, but the guy putting the thing together forgot to look at the school calendar until it was too late. He had planned his blowout event to happen . . . on prom night. Since 80 percent of his students came from the school that was throwing the prom, his event was pretty much doomed.

SEASONS AND TIMING

Good timing—and a bit of horse sense—is very helpful. Most seasoned youth workers will tell you that there are good times and poor times to try to reach teens through outreach events or to start some new ministry expansion.

Christmas season is deadly to most youth groups. Some places, such as in desert communities, virtually close down in the heat of summer, while others are abuzz with kids at that time. Each area has a rhythm of its own: a season when teens are easy to reach and periods when students are preoccupied with school schedules, vacation season or other travel, or holidays. Learning when to push on the pedal and when to ease back is essential in order not to waste energy, time, and money. That seasons dictate what activities are likely drawing cards for teens should, in most cases, be obvious. (A beach trip in the middle of winter is probably a bad idea, unless you're escaping to a tropical zone—in which case the bad idea becomes a good idea.)

Through the years I've found that fall is a particularly good time of year to make new contacts with students, especially during the weeks leading up to Halloween. Activities that used some element of that holiday to draw in students have worked for us for many years. Costumed events, scavenger hunts, spooky movie nights, and Halloween-themed parties tend to get a strong showing of new kids, probably because they're easy for other kids to "sell" to their friends and because they don't feel like "churchy" activities. Teens in the world need to see that we're not exactly studying the Bible every waking moment, but that we have plenty of fun—while putting the Bible into practice—as well.

Of course, what works best in our environment may be a lead balloon in yours, so use your own experience and observation.

In chapters 9 and 10 I'll provide a whole slew of activities that have great potential to be used as drawing cards. With a little creativity, many of them can be retooled to fit nearly any holiday season.

TRUTH FROM THE TRENCHES

Each region of a country has a rhythm of its own: a season when teens are easy to reach and periods when students are preoccupied with school schedules, vacation season or other travel, or holidays.

RUNWAYS

Strategic church planners look for what they call runways upon which to launch their ministries. A runway is a length of time—weeks or months—when people are available without much distraction, including periods that don't coincide with serious holiday breaks. These runways allow a ministry to get speed and lift.

For example, we've found that the first couple of weeks of a new school season are a miserable time to do anything with students. Many parents are trying to start the school year off right by enforcing early curfews and cracking down by insisting that their kids do homework each night. In addition, the teens seem both excited and distracted by the newness of the school year.

A few weeks later, everything usually calms down and turns back to the old routines. This is when we've had intense but powerful runs through early to mid-fall, including the Halloween season, before dropping off just before Thanksgiving. (I'm talking about attendance, new visitors, and overall excitement.) We've experienced similar but less intense runways from mid-January through early May (except for the spring break period). After that, everything has started falling apart again because of graduation season and the summer.

TRUTH FROM THE TRENCHES

Finding runway periods for effective programming launches can allow a youth ministry to get needed speed and lift.

Related thought: avoid trying to use the runway concept at the end of a runway period. For example, having a big ski trip just before Christmas break is probably not going to come off that well. While the activity might draw kids, the follow-up gatherings or events are less likely to be attended because of the busy Christmas season. By the time the holiday is over, the effervescent effect of the ski trip and the potential new relationships coming from it may well be gone. Better to schedule the ski trip where the momentum created can help build interest and enthusiasm.

Seasons when drawing teens is difficult are in some ways blessings in disguise. As those who surf sometimes say about the ocean's unpredictability, "There are times when you need to be out surfing, and there are times where you're better off just to clean the beach."

As our church developed its strategy for reaching teenagers through the years, we decided that some seasons were for going after new teens and pushing growth, and some were for building relationships and doing small group ministries. The nature of this kind of pacing is very different from place to place. The one constant is that every area has a rhythm and wise youth workers will work hard to figure out what it is.

ACTION PLAN

★ What's the seasonal rhythm of your region? In what periods will ministry launches (runways) work well? What periods are best to avoid?

MAKING IT WORK BY CREATING HIGH-QUALITY YOUTH MEETINGS AND EVENTS

Events and meetings are the social settings where good things get done:

★ We get to make new contacts for closer, more personal work.
★ The majority of Bible teaching or evangelistic opportunities takes place.
★ The dynamics of a young community of faith are formed.
★ Teens get a taste of what being part of a church is like.
★ Teens experience a lasting imprint of what being a Christian is like.

Youth meetings and events need to be thought out and crafted well. They need to compete favorably with what the world is offering, not necessarily same-for-same, but in our level of uniqueness and creativity. (Attempting to copy the world and just add Christian icing is generally a bad idea and almost always a losing game.)

TRUTH FROM THE TRENCHES

Attempting to copy the world and just add Christian icing is generally a bad idea and almost always a losing game.

TIPS TO ATTRACT

Here are some tips to consider as you put together any weekly meeting or event that you hope will attract and keep students who at this point in their lives have little or no motivation to be part of a church.

You may have some stuff to lose

To be attractive to outsiders, you may need to toss a few things overboard and get a little more spit and polish going shipboard. Think of it this way: when visitors come to your home, you make sure the place looks inviting, clean, and cheerful. You make sure the dirty clothes are in the hamper, the dishes are out of the sink, and the dog smells good. Your family may have a somewhat different standard of living among yourselves, but when visitors come over you lose some of the sloppy stuff or family oddities—such as cleaning toenails in the living room. You just don't do it.

In the same way, you're inviting in young people who are, in many ways, visitors to your faith community. (You may want to keep your weird uncles and strange family junk stuffed away for a while. Or their visit may be short.) Keep it real, genuine, authentic.

Lose the cheese

A lot of things that youth groups do would fit the urban definition of cheesy—tacky, of poor quality, artless, and inauthentic. Be aware of the cheese factor in your publicity, meeting place, music choices, and the format of your meetings. If anything comes off corny or amateurish, teens are likely to hesitate stepping in. Of course, what's cheesy to one person is cool to another, but most of us know cheesy when we see it. (The middle-age guy with his shirt half opened to reveal his hairy chest and lots of gold chains is cheesy—even if he thinks it's cool.)

Pay attention to what's going on in the youth culture: the images, art style, music, and more. Ask your students—they usually know what's cheesy and what's cool. Tapping a few college-age students to get their help with design and vibe can be another resource. When you involve artistic young people in the creation of materials, stickers, and T-shirts, you keep out cheese and create ownership. (No artists? Visit the folks at www.churchartworks.com and check out their very hip material.)

The exception to the cheese rule is when you're trying for kitsch. For example, we threw a disco party where tacky was the rule; it worked. Being intentionally cheesy can, at times, be cool.

Lose the weirdness

Some churches regularly do things that most people outside the church think are just plain weird. And I'm not just talking about those who are into snake handling; I'm talking about people who think that having everyone hold hands to pray is cool, or actually encouraging group hugs.

Now I have nothing against group hugs—in theory at least. But I know that if I were a new kid in a group of strangers who wanted me to start hugging people I didn't really know, I would be weirded out. (Unless all the huggers were really cute girls, which would mean that you've arrived at young guy heaven.)

Christian groups have difficulty gauging their own weirdness to outsiders. After all, we are about the only people left in the nation who get together and sing. Expect that this might seem a tad uncomfortable to some newbies, even if the music is hot. The situation will seem downright terrifying if the music is lousy. Plus, we commonly use code words such as *salvation* and *grace*, which are not used much in modern culture, or even particularly understood.

Making everyone read from a passage of the Bible during a teaching time may not seem too odd to lifers, but doing so could be a weird (even frightening? horrible?) experience for many teens who've never held a Bible before—let alone trying to get their tongues around cool words such as *propitiation* (an older Bible word that doesn't appear in many of the newer versions) or clever Bible names like *Jaazaniah*.

I understand well the tendency to resist changing or modifying what we consider normal or even necessary church activities in order to ease the passage into Christian community. But a better way to do this is to carefully consider what events or meetings you push to have newcomers experience, and let them gradually ease into understanding the Christian faith. This is far better than plunging them into areas beyond their depth. To go on with this thought . . .

Lose the routine

Many Christian groups have comfortable routines that are so normal to them that they never think about how a person unfamiliar with the trappings of faith might feel. For example, many times a leader may ask his students to turn to a passage in the Bible and church kids start thumbing right away, at least knowing which direction to go. But for an unchurched teen the Bible is a huge mystery—that can be a good thing, when you think about it—and to navigate it is difficult and potentially embarrassing. Printing out or projecting the verses is better for newcomers. Or, if thumbing through the Bible is actually needed, you may want to consider our solution. We bought Bibles to be used in meetings and gave them away to kids. When we asked for a verse to be referenced, we gave the page number as well.

TRUTH FROM THE TRENCHES

Carefully consider what events or meetings you push to have newcomers experience, and let them gradually ease into understanding the Christian faith.

Some of your routines may need to be revisited or reworked to factor in the new teens who don't have the background, attention span, or skills that your regular youth group members have.

How would you design a camp that had 60 percent unchurched kids in attendance? Would some routines need to be changed or altered? Would we need to do a better job explaining our Christian words? Would we stick to our curriculum plan, or rework it to make it applicable to those who have very little background in faith?

Be aware of first impressions

As everyone knows, you only get one chance to make a first impression. So what do you think the average newbie thinks when he or she stumbles into your meeting or event?

The first impression of the entire situation begins to set their minds toward what they'll think about you and your group. Subtle things give powerful messages. Is the room clean, orderly, and yet interesting looking? Or does it smell of mildew or unemptied trash? (Churches are notorious for sticking the youth in the basement.) Does it have a friendly, make-you-want-to-hang-out feel? Or is it sterile, cluttered, or as appealing as a thrift store? (Which is very common, as many youth rooms are littered with cast-off sofas and furniture.)

TRUTH FROM THE TRENCHES

Subtle things give powerful messages. Is your youth room clean, orderly, and yet interesting looking? Or does it smell of mildew or unemptied trash? First impressions count for a lot.

For a terrific example of strong thinking about first impressions and creating a welcoming environment, I suggest a quick study of Disneyland. The designers of that California theme park have been studying people for decades. The average church could learn a thing or two from what they've discovered.

For example, Disney's planners found that people would only hold on to their trash for 27 feet on average, and then they would lay it down. Somewhere. Anywhere. To keep their park clean, Disney made sure to have trash cans no farther than 27 feet apart. (And they empty them regularly.)

The park is designed so that people go where Disneyland wants them to go, not where they might otherwise go. Initially, Disneyland had sidewalks with lots of right angles. They found that people cut across the flower beds rather than follow the sidewalks, even when little fences were erected. So, they ripped up the flower beds and sidewalks and made everything go with the natural flow of how people walked through the park. No right angles.

Disneyland's Main Street has a lot of food shops. Somebody figured out that by blowing the scent of heated vanilla out the window, the enticing aroma would trigger something in people racing for the rides that screamed, "Hey, stop for something to eat!"

First impressions are huge at Disneyland because they want you to enjoy yourself and come back. Kind of like what we want with our youth groups.

Grow your friendliness factor

Not only are a visitor's first impressions based on ambience, they're largely based on how welcoming the environment is. This is often a tougher nut to crack. We can control the physical environment, but the friendliness of teens is ultimately up to them.

Christian groups, like any other collection of teens, can be filled with cliques that are difficult to break into. So you may want to work with your regular crew before launching into a major event that might attract newcomers to the group.

This may not be for every group, but we tried something with our students to help them see the importance of stepping up to welcome new teens. We worked with a student from another church who was unknown to our kids; that person acted as a secret "visitor"—the same way stores sometimes have secret shoppers who pretend to shop but are really evaluating the warmth of the employees. Our secret visitor was instructed to be a little shy but to respond when spoken to. In particular, we wanted to find out if many kids would go out of their way to make our friend feel welcomed.

We timed the visit to coincide with a session dealing with friendship evangelism. At the end of the meeting, we unveiled our plot and let the chips fall. It was a powerful and even painful moment for the teens in our group, but it helped to prepare and motivate them for other visitors who might find their way into the group. (By the way, a number of churches and adult ministries have done similar things, and any initial anger on the part of members about the ploy is almost always replaced by a sense of learning from the experience, and by personal conviction.)

We even traded secret visitors with other youth groups whose leaders heard about our experiment!

Know your flock

Accumulate some background material on visitors as soon as is reasonable. This will give you a context in which to understand and work with them. Use a short questionnaire. Here's a sample form:

Name: ....

Address: ....

....

Phone (home or cell): ....

Grade, school: ....

E-mail: ....

Do you live with: ❑ both parents ❑ one parent

                    ❑ split time between parents?

                    ❑ family member other than parent(s)

Who are two or three of your best friends at this church?

....

What are one or two things you most enjoy doing as a

sport, hobby, or pastime?...

....

Name some bands or music you enjoy: ....

....

Name one or two of your favorite movies: ....

....

What's your favorite/least favorite subjects in school?

....

What's your favorite video game, reality show, cartoon,

or cereal? (You choose!)..

ONRAMP IDEAS THAT ATTRACT

I'm always looking for a new way to connect with secular teens. I call these ideas onramps as they're designed to ease teens into our communities of faith the same way you ease your car out onto the highway. Sometimes onramps are remarkably simple, easy, cheap, and effective.

Think games that guys—and girls—will love

Before safety advocates put an end to it, any store that sold toys bristled with dart guns. Not the weak, stubby, flexible darts that are sold today but the old-fashioned, suction-cup-on-a-stiff-plastic-rod kind in a spring-loaded gun. When shot, those darts really took off and had a decent wallop. They were cheap. A gun and six darts. I bought about fifty of them, and a new game was born: Dart Wars.

We played at night, usually after 9:00. We played in the church building, with all the doors propped open and any rooms where no play was allowed (such as the pastor's office) locked. We played in the dark. No lights were allowed during play. One team hid. The other team, starting from the only room with a light on, went out to find them—creeping silently through the darkened rooms. (If you play a game like this, to protect your church's liability, have the kids wear goggles.)

If you were hit you had to declare it, discontinue the fight, and return to the morgue (the room with the light on) to suck on sodas until your team all passed away or became victorious. Meanwhile, survivors scrambled around in the dark listening for breathing and scratching the floor for spent darts to add to their arsenal.

Dart Wars was simple, dumb, easy—and absolutely, unbelievably popular. New kids flocked to it, and I found out that sitting in the morgue talking to the "casualties" was a great way to get to know new kids. We would play Dart

Wars every weekend evening and many weekdays as well. (I can recall sitting in church and seeing a bright orange dart missed from the cleanup of the previous evening stuck on the wall above the pulpit.)

At this very moment there are men and women who, when asked to tell the story of their conversion to Christ, will start by saying, "Well, there was this church that played a game in the dark with dart guns . . . "

Sadly, I can no longer find the darts of this kind. I can tell you my honest thought whenever I can't find this product is: Curse you, safety advocates!

As this illustration shows, you don't need a bunch of money or huge amounts of time and energy to come up with something that really grabs secular teens and stokes your regular crew too. The key is creating an event or environment where teens want to come to us. When kids come willingly, even anxiously, to our turf, we can call the shots and set the expectations.

TRUTH FROM THE TRENCHES

You don't need a bunch of money or huge amounts of time and energy to come up with something that really grabs secular teens and stokes your regular crew too. The key is creating an event or environment where teens want to come to us.

So lame it's cool

I'm always on the lookout for ideas that work with teens. As I said earlier, not all ideas have to be slick, hip, and state of the art to attract. Some of them can be so silly that they turn into attractive fun.

For example, while roaming the aisles at a Wal-Mart store, I noticed a huge collection of ridiculous inflatable pool toys—whales, sharks, turtles, and a lot more. The dumb stuff gave me the idea of having an Inflatable Day at our local beach; the object would be to go out into the surf not with surfboards, bodyboards, or anything cool, but with silly pool toys. Inflatable Day has turned into one of the most fun annual events that we do with teens. They turn up with their air mattresses, pool toys, and inner tube rings and clog up the beach.

I've seen similar lame things retooled to be terrific draws. For example, as I write, the big rage with our high school students is dodgeball. We have a dodgeball league, official T-shirts, official refs, and a huge turnout at every Dodgeball Night. This has created the need for a bit of revamping of our game room. Steel shutters have been put in place in front of the windows. The dodgeball league has taken off, and at the end of every session the gospel message is delivered by one of the players or team leaders.

GETTING REAL BANG FOR THE BUCK

A word of caution: groups often invest lots of energy and money into outreach events that, in truth, get very little return. (*Return*, here, equaling impact and connection with unbelievers.)

For example, a concert with big-name performers costs a lot of money when fees, publicity, travel, hotels, and food are factored in. While the concert may draw a good-sized group of teens, other than a nice experience and possibly a few cool words about Jesus, it's a lot of work and money for a fairly small end result. (And this is assuming the concert is well attended.)

This is not to discourage hosting concerts, but we need to find a way to get more mileage from these events through things like collecting names and addresses—having a raffle ticket that teens fill out is one idea—or promoting an upcoming event on the heels of the concert. Also, when we host a concert, we often ask whether one of our local bands can open with a few songs, which make our little bands feel like big stuff.

We've found that it's sometimes in our better interest to grab teens and take them to the concert of a big-name performer rather than try to host one ourselves.

In addition, we'll often have lesser-known bands do concerts as the economic risk is far less, and many kids like the idea of being on the first rung of popularizing an upcoming band. (Kind of like saying, "Yeah, I hung out with U2 when they played the little clubs.")

The same caution is true for activities such as snowboard trips, houseboat weekends, and the like. Some of these activities, while popular and attractive to outsiders, must be approached with a strong dose of realism about what can be accomplished.

For example, during a snowboard trip, kids scatter in small groups for the whole day and come back tired and burned out. They may sit still for an evening Bible study or talk, but half of them will probably nod off. Any attempts to crimp back on getting to the slopes in order to have a meeting will be met with silent contempt and a hurry-and-get-this-over-with attitude. Not exactly an atmosphere that is soul nurturing.

In addition, these kinds of activities are very expensive.

Again, I'm not suggesting that snowboard or ski trips shouldn't be done. But I would suggest that there are a myriad of other things that can be done easier, cheaper, and with better results. A big, flashy outreach effort might be less effective than a smaller, better thought-out endeavor.

TRUTH FROM THE TRENCHES

Big, flashy outreach efforts often turn out less effective than smaller, better thought-out endeavors.

CAMPS

Almost all kids love to get away from home, and a camp situation (retreat center or roughing it) is both attractive and potentially powerful in making personal and spiritual connections.

Some areas have professionally run retreat center camps where all that's required from the youth worker is to show up with the youth group and counselors. In other areas, if there is a camp facility, it's one that you have to rent out and arrive at with your own cooks and program staff, as well as counselors. Naturally, the latter types of camps are a lot more work but also can be customized much easier.

The thing that makes a camping situation ripe with possibilities is that it is usually carefully designed to create a spiritual environment for a number of days. Personal relationships are forged between students and students, and students and adult counselors; the entire week affords breaks from typical daily routines; and the challenge of faith offered at camp meetings is almost always uplifting.

A remarkable number of students make decisions for Christ during camping events.

If you're not familiar with good Christian camps in your area talk to other youth workers or check out the resources available near you at Christian Camp and Conference Association (www.ccca.org).

For ideas on themes, games, and how to create and wisely operate your own camp, check out the resources offered by organizations like Youth Specialties and Group Publishing, and here are two more specific resources: *Camp Themes & Games* (at www.unkommonmedia.com) and, for camps for teen girls, Standard Publishing's *One Girl Leader's Guide* (www.standardpub.com).

DECISION TIME

Billy Graham was known for inviting those who wanted to become believers to leave their seats ("the buses will wait") and come to the foot of the stage. What many people don't know about his crusades is that, generally, the first group of people who left the seats was the pre-assigned counselors who were making their way to the floor in order to talk with potential converts (as well as to encourage the timid by seeing others head down the steps). So, for many, coming forward at an altar call or raising their hands to signify a willingness to believe have become two of the primary ways that a decision for Christ must be made.

But these are merely methods and certainly not biblical dictates. Methods that worked well at one point in history or with one group of people do not necessarily work in another time and place.

While you need to clearly present the core message of hope and forgiveness by Christ's sacrifice on the cross, there are numerous ways to help young people come to a point of decision in accepting the good news. One of the most effective seems to be offering them a time to quietly be alone with God, without peers, without pressure from a speaker, and yet assisted, if needed, on the decision they may need to take. Standing alone in a dark, open field for a five-minute discipline of silence can do wonders for a young person's heart as he or she is on the brink of this decision.

Decision time is not about closing the sale. It's not getting scalps or keeping score of souls swishing into the bucket of eternity. It is allowing teens (or any person, for that matter) the dignity of hearing God's call and being able to choose entirely for themselves.

Carefully crafting that opportunity is vital.

TRUTH FROM THE TRENCHES

Decision time is not about closing the sale. It's not getting scalps or keeping score of souls swishing into the bucket of eternity.

You may find that most decisions to follow Christ do not come as a result of an organized outreach opportunity but rather as a quiet commitment of faith made individually, student by student. While there is no magic formula in how to move a seeker to faith, there's also no harm in giving some clarity to teens who are considering putting their faith in Christ. Explain clearly what being a Christian means, and if you get an opportunity to pray with the young person as they seek God more deeply and consider a decision, then consider it a blessing.

ACTION PLAN

★ What are some onramp ideas, games, or other activities that you've never tried that could be used to effectively reach teens who are visiting your ministry?

MAKING IT WORK: IDEAS FOR OUTREACH

Most of these ideas are onramps that will draw kids to you and your church.

GAME NIGHTS

Game nights are forty-five minutes of mayhem culminating in a short but inviting message. For a game night to work right you'll need:

★ space to run around—a gym or large empty room
★ some really cool games (of course)
★ props and prizes (cheap bags of candy to shower on a winning team)
★ a mic or public address of some kind to give instructions
★ staff, preferably trained to set up, tear down, clean up, and help with games
★ transportation (most likely to and from)
★ a "take home" table loaded up with free Bibles, promotional material, and any other goodies you can get into the hands of teens for spiritual growth or consideration
★ as with nearly all events, a way to get info from visiting teens for mailing, phone, or texting

Keys to making a game night fun

Those are the physical things you'll need. But here are the keys to making these nights really rock:

★ Use games that everyone can play. Stunts and skits are OK once in awhile, but kids disengage if they're not playing.

★ Have clear, easy-to-follow rules. The more complex the game, the more likely it will fail. Mark all boundaries clearly with tape, lights, or whatever you need. Mark your teams as well; boundary tape or colored duct tape are great tools to use so that everyone can see who's a teammate and who's an opponent. Use a whistle to signal starts and stops. And make sure everyone knows playing is mandatory—otherwise, girls will sit on the sideline and chew gum or text.

★ Have your props ready to go. Nothing stalls a game night more than having to wait around for props to be created or set up.

★ Make the competition even. For example, line up your teens from tallest to small-est (boys, then girls) and choose your teams by going down the line. The object is to get an equal mix of big and small kids on each team; otherwise, the big guys wipe out the small ones.

★ As we've discussed, aim your games toward males; make them fast, active, and physical. And remember that in middle school girls can give as good as they get, so don't worry too much about the princesses.

★ Try coming up with game night themes to make this more fun: Jell-O Night, Glow in the Dark Night, Toilet Night, and lots more that your creativity will provide you with.

★ Keep the pace quick. Teens will be much harder to pull back together if there's a lot of dead time between games. Have staff working on game setup or cleanup while you give the instructions for the next game.

★ Take photos or video of the action and project them before the next game night starts.

★ Set up a sound system and use music while the games are in progress. Make the whole thing feel like a TV production.

★ Keep a first aid kit handy, along with lots of cleaning supplies. You'll likely need them.

★ Keep your message short and fast-paced. Teens are usually hot, sweaty, and keyed up after playing the games. At a game night, nobody has ever complained about a message that's too short.

TRUTH FROM THE TRENCHES

A game night must have clear, easy-to-follow rules. The more complex the game, the more likely it will fail.

AIRSOFT WARS

Airsoft guns are a somewhat milder version of BB guns that shoot small plastic pellets instead of steel. A church campus is a great place to have an Airsoft war as there are plenty of rooms and things to hide behind. The downside to an Airsoft spree is the residue of pellets that get scattered everywhere. (Plan on having lots of strong vacuums on hand for cleanup time.)

Masks or goggles are a must for Airsoft. (You can shoot an eye out!) You might want to supply the guns to keep the playing field even, as some kids may show up with some serious weaponry.

Boys in particular flock to Airsoft wars and love to show off the tiny welts they get in battle.

It goes without saying that there should be no other events scheduled on campus while having an Airsoft war! And by the way, this activity works equally well with either middle school or high school students.

DRIVING LESSONS

Disclaimer up front: For this one, you'll need to have the permission of parents and a safe place to do this activity. (The church parking lot can be ideal.)

And you should be a patient kind of person because you'll get some kids who will really test you behind the wheel of your car.

Sometimes the most simple of ideas are overlooked for the more glamorous ones.

One easy way to meet new teens and make friends is to offer driving lessons, particularly teaching teens how to parallel park (with cones, not cars) and how to use a clutch.

Most of us have been driving so long that we forget the thrill of getting behind the wheel for the first few times and how fearful we were of not being able to pass our driver's test. Or we forget the fear we felt of embarrassment at the possibility of jerking down the street because we had no idea how to drive a manual shift car.

You can be a hero to a small crew of teens by making your vehicle the sacrificial lamb to their driving aspirations. Oh—and be willing to install a new clutch in your car a bit earlier than you'd planned.

MOVIE MAKING

Every kid loves to see herself or himself on the screen, especially if they're doing something noteworthy. Capitalize on this instinct by grabbing a video camera and shooting the action of kids doing something energetic. (Or find someone who has talent with a camcorder and editing software, and you act as the director.)

For example, by going to a local skate park and filming a bunch of the groms soaring, crashing, and whipping off ramps, you have an easy transition to inviting them all to see the edited version of the movie on the big screen at church. (Complete with popcorn, soda, and hot music.) Few will turn down a chance to see themselves in action, especially if you put their names on the screen as they skate.

I know how well this works. This was what brought me to youth group after a surf trip where my smooth moves were filmed. Heck, I was so confident of my surfing that I brought a few other friends along with me to witness my starring role. (Which the youth worker wisely showed after a short Bible talk.)

If you want to go even deeper into movie making as an outreach tool, try creating your own parody film. Use any easy-to-costume action film: *Robin Hood, Zorro,* westerns, horror, pirate, *Lord of the Rings, Star Trek, Star Wars,* and plenty more. These epics can involve large amounts of kids in both starring and supporting roles. Create a non-dialogue script for a fifteen-to-twenty minute movie. (I suggest using a voice-over narration to tell your story, as having kids say lines is difficult and time consuming.) Make your story corny, silly, and outrageous with lots of sight gags. Keep special effects to a minimum. If you decide to shoot on location, you can even make the film while at a retreat.

We created a horror movie that managed to have zombies, the Wolfman, Dracula, Frankenstein's monster, and Mr. Hyde—all in the same flick.

With help from people who are a whiz at filming and editing, you can create a blockbuster that's lots of fun to make.

And making it is only half the fun. The premier night is even better—especially if you bring in a red carpet, rent a limo (have it drive around in circles picking up new "stars" each trip), create Oscar awards, and lampoon Hollywood in any other way possible. Of course, parents and friends will show up in droves. With any luck, your ticket, DVD, and popcorn sales will help make up the cost of your movie. (Our last film cost $2,000 due to the props, costumes, and other goodies—but the results were worth the expense!)

This is not just a fun activity. The potential of this project to get you into places—such as the public schools—is huge. Students who are willing to approach teachers often find that their teachers are more than willing to have the director (that's you) come into the class to show the movie and discuss how the film was made. This is a perfect opportunity to not only explain the film but also some of the other cool things you're doing for teens who want to have fun.

We've seen the attendance at our middle school midweek meeting double virtually every time we go on campus with a new movie—no exaggeration. Teens are always looking for something new and creative to do. And their fellow students treated all the kids who appeared in the film as stars—at least for a day.

CAMPUS BIBLE CLUBS

Many public schools allow students to host a campus Bible club at some time before or after school. For the most part, campus Bible studies are merely a holy huddle with little impact on the campus as a whole. Not that Christians getting together is bad, but unless you help your kids, many times the thought of using the club for evangelistic purposes never crosses their minds. But with motivated student leaders, a little creativity, and some help from adults, a Bible club often has the potential to do some meaningful things in spreading the word among peers.

Here is some of what I've seen Bible clubs do:

★ Create and distribute free book covers that are designed not only to be attractive but to contain appropriate Scripture references—sort of like an attractive tract that you use to cover your books. (Since they are handed out by students from an officially sanctioned club, few schools will challenge this activity and many students will find themselves noodling on the words during some boring class.)

★ Create a prom event for special education class members. These can be fabulous, garner the right kind of attention for your church, and be one of the most uplifting activities of your entire year.

★ Provide teachers with a special luncheon as a way to say thank you.

★ Take out a page in the yearbook that contains an attractive design with an invitation to the Bible club or your church.

★ Host a Christian rock band on campus during lunch, with invites to a concert in the evening.

★ Hand out hot chocolate and donuts on a cold morning to students as they get off the bus, or at bus stops.

A little creative thinking often spurs students to come up with ideas that will make an impact on their fellow students, with possible eternal results. And yes, some of the ideas our students came up with took funds, which is where the local church stepped in and made a donation to the Campus Christian Club.

TRUTH FROM THE TRENCHES

With motivated student leaders, a little creativity, and some help from adults, a campus Bible club has the potential to do some meaningful things in spreading the word among peers.

ROCK 'EM

Teens love rock music. There is nothing quite so exciting to a lot of teens as sliding behind a drum kit or strapping a lean electric guitar on their backs. But for teens trying to put together a little band, there is often not much more than a lot of frustration.

Teens usually have to practice in the garage, and even then the neighbors complain and parents yell to "Turn it down!" While some young, aspiring musicians may have some gear, most don't have a sound system or even heavy-duty amps. Then, even if they are able to put a band together, the opportunities to play are usually limited.

Teens in your area in rock bands might have a new best friend: your church. Many churches have ample-sized rooms that bands can use to rehearse, and there often are a number of nights or afternoons where the facilities are not being used. In addition, churches often have great sound systems and many have a full array of amps, drum kits, and other musical marvels.

Another plus is that if a band is made up of teens in the youth group, the congregation is likely to support them and become a sort of fan base. If the musicians show skill, very likely they'll be drafted into a worship band or allowed a slot in "big church" as well as the youth group.

Naturally, to get permission to bring in head-banging kids from the outside to scream lyrics into valuable church gear will take a bit of political maneuvering, some careful monitoring of those teens, and some help from sound people and other musicians. But using the means of music and the space and gear of the church to connect with kids from the outside is a powerful tool for outreach.

We went a step further and created a weekend event that's designed to sharpen the musical chops for teens in and out of the church. We call it Rock 'N U, and it's focused in particular on rock music. Using professional rock musicians (we bring in a couple of bands) and local talent, we offer seminars and breakout sessions in about every aspect of playing rock 'n' roll, from increasing music skills on drum, bass, or guitar to managing sound systems, exploring recording, crafting songs, and even leading worship.

Interlínc is a well-known company that creates music-based resources for youth ministry. The organization has developed an extensive guide on how to help ministries get music and media going. You can check them out at http://interlinc-online.com/.

TRUTH FROM THE TRENCHES

Using music and the space and gear of the church to connect
with teens from the outside is a powerful tool for outreach.

HALLOWEEN

If your congregation has the openness to bringing in jack-o'-lanterns, various
monsters, and ghosts for a short season, you may find the holiday that wraps up
the month of October as one of the better opportunities to draw in teens who are
looking for a place to do a couple of simple things: have fun and dress silly.

We've had terrific results using everything from spooky themes (tongue in
cheek, of course) to plenty of black and orange decorations to pull off some
of the following:

★ Scavenger or treasure hunts: Teams are put together with a list of objectives and a
time limit. Things on the list can be fun but "creepy" items such as a live spider, a
slug, a fake finger nail, dog hair, and more—all of which are needed ingredients
for the witch's cauldron.

★ Costume parties: Encourage creativity and imagination with prizes. Don't worry,
you can require that there be no sleazy costumes. Do your costume judging before
you start any games or party fun. Take lots of photos and post them later.

★ Glow in the dark fun: get your hands on lots of glow in the dark necklaces and toys
and play all kinds of games in the dark.

★ Spooky Movie Night: Be extremely wise here and research well before making a
choice—some of the teen horror flicks are full of trash. Look for a classic that's
creepy but without the flesh and gore. Ask your students; many will know what to
get. If your parents will allow it, start the show at midnight.

DRIVING TEENS HOME

"When will you be home tonight?" my wife asked.

"I dunno," I said. "I'm going to drive some of the kids home tonight after the meeting."

"Don't you have staff that will do that?" she asked.

"Yeah, but do you remember that kid who I had such a heavy talk with last week because he was hurting from his grandma's sudden death?"

"I remember," she said with a smile. "I'll be waiting for you."

"Eyes closed or open?" I asked.

Welcome to my life.

Everything that follows should be seen and understood through the filter of male youth workers driving the guys home and the women taking the girls. The point is, you don't want to be alone in the car, at night, with a teen of the opposite sex. But truthfully, you should be even further above board than that. Make sure you have two youth workers in the car, or, if driving by yourself, two teens that you drop off together at the final residence. The point is, avoid one adult and one teen (even of the same sex) together in a car.

At first glance, the task of taking teens home after a meeting or event hardly seems like an outreach opportunity. But after many decades in youth work I'd have to say that the conversations that take place as I drive teens to their homes are far more insightful, penetrating, and spiritually charged than most of the dialogue that went on in that evening's Bible study.

The problem is that these kinds of conversations are tricky. They can't be staged, they can't be planned or even anticipated, and most often they last for only a few minutes, until some clown wrecks the mood.

But while they last, they are golden.

So if these opportunities are so elusive, why even bring it up here? Because I want to make sure that you're alert to the opportunity and then looking for how to stack the deck in your favor so that great dialogue has the potential to take place.

What do I mean by stack the deck? Make sure that you take home last the kids who you want to talk with. (You may have to choose a creative driving route.) You also stack the deck by making sure you're skilled at asking questions that are personal in nature, but not so personal that they're scary, overly intrusive, or could even be construed as crossing the line.

For example, asking about parents and siblings is fine. Hobbies, sports, favorite games, or movies are safe as well. Watch for the cracks where you can probe a little deeper. "So, you said your parents are divorced—who do you live with?" . . . "Do you see your dad (or mom) very often?" . . . "How do you feel about that?" If the divorce was a long time ago or if there was never a marriage, chances are the student sees their situation as normal since this is all they've ever known. If the divorce was recent or is in the works, you can be sure that you have a hurting puppy on your hands and that they would love a chance to express their thoughts and feelings to someone who cares.

A car ride home is a chance to tell interesting little stories about yourself that allow teens to feel a closer bond, very possibly sparking a deeper discussion. "Yeah, when I was twelve, I was bit by a rattlesnake and almost died!" is an example of the kind of discussion-starter that will get everyone in the car talking. Any adventure, accident, hardship, or misadventure that we can mine from our lives is helpful to open hearts and mouths. And these can include the perfect opportunity to tell the story of how we came to faith in Christ.

Keep in mind that these opportunities may be precursors to other conversations where the students themselves bring up questions of faith. There have been many times I've pulled my car off the road to keep an intense discussion going rather than have it quelled by reaching the home destination before we wrapped up the talk.

The potential for great conversations is one reason I make sure to drive students home after every meeting or event. Yes, I could have volunteers do the driving, but I'd rather use them to shut down the facilities so I can spend time with teens in this quieter venue. I allow for the extra half hour to hour to haul teens from our meeting place to their homes, and consider it a continuation of the connection process from the meeting or event.

TRUTH FROM THE TRENCHES

A car ride home with teens is a chance to tell interesting little stories about yourself that allow them to feel a closer bond, very possibly sparking a deeper discussion.

ACTION PLAN

★ What outreach ideas given in this chapter have the greatest potential in your ministry? How could you get them started? What obstacles will you need to overcome?

MAKING IT WORK: ORDER, CONTROL, AND DISCIPLINE AMONG ROGUES

A key element in making effective outreach work is the ability to manage and control the scoundrels that you may collect in the process. Strong leaders tend to lead. This is fine if you can get them to lead in the direction you desire—and an absolute disaster if they lead against you.

I've found a few key concepts helpful in making sure that my staff and I control the environment.

A STRONG STAFF LEADER: YOU NEED A BULL

This is generally you—but if not, you'll need to make sure you have a "bull" on your team who can ensure everything goes the way you want. (Note: You should never need to intimidate a rebellious teen, but having someone who they're just a bit fearful to cross is very helpful in the toughest of situations.)

The need to establish who is the authority from the start (without coming off like a drill instructor) is extremely important, especially if you're starting to attract street kids for whom the idea of authority is a foreign one.

How? Well, say it clearly. "This is my show, and these are my reasonable rules. We'll all have a good time if we play within the lines."

I suggest that your youth group run like a benevolent dictatorship, with you being the smiling, happy, upbeat dictator.

TRUTH FROM THE TRENCHES

The need to establish who is the authority from the start (without coming off like a drill instructor) is extremely important, especially if you're starting to attract street kids for whom the idea of authority is a foreign one.

PREEMPTIVE THINKING

The vast majority of disruptive problems that take place come from the leader not thinking in advance and not doing simple things that can defuse potential problems.

Look around the meeting area. Are there things your teens will get their hands on and play with when they should be involved with something else? Are there distractions that will prove too attractive for a teenager to avoid? (A chair with wheels, for example. You can pretty much bet that at least a couple of teens will fight over the stupid thing, and the victor will roll around the room throughout your meeting—if you let him.) Eliminating these items before your teens get on site will save the hassle of having to take them away, in front of other kids, later.

A sofa in a youth meeting room is usually a constant source of friction. Take care of this beforehand either by removing the sofa or getting a whole bunch more.

Teenagers, both of the secular and Christian varieties, will sometimes argue about seating or who gets what bunk at camp.

For decades, I've used a simple method that has served to preempt these kinds of squabbles. We call it Age Has Priority. That's it. The oldest gets their choice. Of course, this is completely unfair to the younger ones or those who get there first, but the seniors in the group love it and it does give the younger teens something to look forward to in years to come.

Preemptive thinking works in many, many situations. For example, if I'm taking kids camping, I usually go to the location ahead of time, scout out the lay of the land, find where the bathrooms are located, and determine the places where kids will try to sneak off to after lights out—so I can be there waiting for them.

I want to go into situations with the advantage; it gives me quiet authority among the students.

Make sure to clearly explain rules and boundaries to students before you launch an event, activity, or outing. Do not presume your knuckleheads know what those boundaries are, especially if they come from backgrounds where discipline is loose and boundaries arbitrary or nonexistent.

TRUTH FROM THE TRENCHES

When it comes to control, go into your events with the advantage. It will give you quiet authority among the students.

All rules and expectations should be thought out in advance whenever possible and should be kept simple. For example, I could make a huge list of meeting room rules: no pinching, no pulling hair, no burping, no making odd noises, no flipping your eyelids, and many more. Or I could simply say, "Don't do anything that disturbs the learning of another person."

That little rule covers just about everything.

You also need to clearly explain that there will be consequences for violating the rules, but you don't have to always explain exactly what the consequences will be. For example, if you say "no drugs or alcohol" at an activity, what happens if someone pushes the limits? Not setting a predetermined rule gives you latitude to make decisions that are in the best interest of the group and the violator. On top of that, all violations are different and will probably need differing consequences.

By the way, you should do all of this with a smile on your face.

TRUTH FROM THE TRENCHES

Establish and keep order among your group with a firm hand—and a smile on your face (at nearly all times).

THE LITTLE THINGS

Subtle things can help with creating an environment that is conducive to order and control. A clean, neat room is more likely to invite order than a messy one. A room that is at a workable temperature makes a discipline situation easier than a room that is too hot or too cold.

Having the proper tools on hand (paper, pencils, Bibles, props, and more), having enough of them, and, of course, being prepared in your delivery, increases the likelihood for order, discipline, and control.

DISCIPLINE

The point of applying discipline is to change behavior; it should never be entered into when we're angry or hot about the stupidity of a teen. Generally speaking, a little bit of discipline goes a long way and can establish a reputation for yourself that can even spread from generation to generation of teen.

As I've stated, I see taking teens home as part of my outreach. Of course, it's also a service to the teen and his family. One night, in the process of taking kids home, we stopped at a mini-mart and I treated the kids to a drink. A new bottled drink was all the rage and a few of the kids bought this new beverage in its hip glass container.

As we were cruising along with windows down on a warm evening, I happened to notice something flash in the side mirror, followed by several loud pops. Two of the kids in the back seat had decided it would be fun to toss their glass bottles out my car window. Glass now littered the neighborhood street, and if any cop had been around, I would have been looking at a hefty ticket.

I pulled the car over and quickly found out who the culprits were.

I was ticked at those two, I'll be honest. But I kept my cool and unemotionally announced that these two clowns had violated my good graces, generosity, and trust—and were no longer invited for a ride home. Then I booted them out of the car. We were more than a mile from their homes, and it was night.

They whimpered and said they were sorry.

I said I was sorry too, but that they had now entered the penalty box from which, tonight, there was no escape. Perhaps they might think differently about what to do with their trash next week when getting a ride home with me, but on this evening, they'd have a nice, brisk walk to contemplate all of these things.

I added, "Oh, by the way, if your parents want to know why you had to walk home, have them call me!" Naturally, I never got a call.

My discipline of these guys was just, quick, appropriate for the crime—and effective. I never had anyone toss stuff out of my car again. And I would sometimes overhear one teenager warning another one: "And don't throw anything out of Rick's car. He'll stop right wherever he is and make you walk home."

A reputation can sometimes be a fine thing to have.

I don't tell this little story to recommend that you regularly kick kids out of your car and make them walk the final mile home at night. In fact, you probably don't want to do that. (In Kauai, it's a bit more rural, and I would do this back in the day.) I tell it to say that there are times when it's appropriate to take more serious action, when it's necessary to really get a teenager's attention.

WHEN TO GET PARENTS INVOLVED

In a typical church setting, when some teen goes off the rails in the behavior department, the parents are invited to the party. But when working with teens outside the church, considerably more tact might be necessary. Does the teen who is in trouble have parents who will overreact or work against the best interest of the student?

I recall busting a kid for drugs but deciding not to involve the parents. The reason? The boy got his drugs from Mom and Dad's stash.

Knowing what you're dealing with is essential. Of course, it goes without saying that any abuse, suicide threats, or other destructive behavior needs to be reported to the proper authorities. (A terrific guide to these kinds of situation is *The Parent's Guide to Helping Teenagers in Crisis*, by Rich Van Pelt and Jim Hancock, Zondervan/Youth Specialties, 2008.)

ACTION PLAN

★ Where have you seen discipline situations where a firm hand has made all the difference? Have you seen situations where lack of planning led to control problems? How can you strengthen your ministry in this area?

MAKING IT WORK THROUGH FAMILY OUTREACH

When Zac first showed up at church, he came primarily because he had become a friend of one of the teens in our youth group. Before long, the message of the gospel became real to him. As he grew in his faith and became more involved in the life of the church (he played in the worship band, among other roles), his parents began noticing the changes in him. Before long, they began to show up on Sundays too. (They had previously been only occasional church attendees.) Within a few years, the entire family had come to Christ and Zac's dad became part of the leadership team.

Zac, at the time of this writing, is serving as a youth pastor at a church on the East Coast.

This example is the poster boy of what we all hope will take place through our efforts to win teenagers. Of course, there are no guarantees. But we must always remember that when we reach out to a young person we're reaching out to his or her entire family as well.

And some of these family situations can be gnarly.

We must guard against being merely teen-focused and not seeing the others with whom this student spends his or her life as worthy of our time and energy as well. There are plenty of ways that you can gently make connections.

For example, host a parents' evening where you introduce yourself and your staff and explain who you are and what you're about. A word of caution: don't expect this event to be heavily attended if you work with teens from unstable home situations. (If food is involved, make sure to get RSVPs.) Our experience has suggested that dysfunctional parents are hard to count on and often have little genuine interest in what their kids are doing. (We tell ourselves that we're doing such a good job that they simply trust us and feel they don't need to come to an introduction event, but we're flattering ourselves when we think this way.)

A letter to the parents of new kids introducing yourself, inviting them to anything that would be appropriate for them (such as a parenting seminar), and giving them the tools to contact you is an important first step.

Encouraging your new teenager to invite younger siblings to kids' programs in the church is another way to extend the outreach you're doing.

The point is that we make sure we're not seeing young people as disconnected from the others involved in their lives, and that we make intentional efforts to invite them to events and continue to communicate with them. It's about making the necessary efforts to bring them into what our family of faith is doing.

For much more on this topic, see a companion book in this series, *Engaging Parents as Allies*, by Wayne Rice.

TRUTH FROM THE TRENCHES

We have to guard against being merely teen-focused and not seeing the others with whom this student spends his or her life as worthy of our time and energy as well. There are plenty of ways that you can gently make connections.

ACTION PLAN

★ Have vision, and faith, for entire families to come to Christ through your work with unchurched teens. Who are some teens visiting your ministry whose parent(s) you can get to know?

A FINAL WORD: FROG KISSERS

Remember the old tale of the enchanted prince who was trapped in the body of a frog and could only be released if he found a princess dumb enough to kiss him? It's a great yarn, but leaves a lot of unanswered questions. For example, what is the true frog-to-hexed-prince ratio? How many would you have to smooch before a prince popped up?

If you have a heart for the unreached teenagers cruising the malls and skate parks, you're probably going to be kissing a lot of frogs. You will be giving your love, your energy, and your attention to teens—with no guarantee that they will respond.

Some will, of course, and those are the teens who will be new, young royalty in God's kingdom.

In some cases, the kiss of love you give them will have a delayed fuse and the actual transformation in their lives will take place far from your knowledge.

You should also be aware that hanging out with lots of frogs may give you your fair share of warts. You might find yourself using their slang, enjoying some froggy music, and not sweating some of the things that once made you sweat.

Loving those who are trapped in their frog world, who often are unaware that they have a life available to them beyond their little lily pad, is a high and noble calling, and one that Jesus modeled so well. One can almost hear the self-righteous guys screeching at Jesus: "But how can you call yourself the Son of God?? You . . . you hang around with . . . amphibians!"

We frog kissers seem to be in good company.

The apostle Paul, chief among toads by his own declaration, gets the final word in this book:

Take a good look, friends, at who you were when you got called into this life. I don't see many of "the brightest and the best" among you, not many influential, not many from high-society families. Isn't it obvious that God deliberately chose men and women that the culture overlooks and exploits and abuses, chose these "nobodies" to expose the hollow pretensions of the "somebodies"? That makes it quite clear that none of you can get by with blowing your own horn before God. Everything that we have—right thinking and right living, a clean slate and a fresh start—comes from God by way of Jesus Christ. That's why we have the saying, "If you're going to blow a horn, blow a trumpet for God."

1 CORINTHIANS 1:26-31, THE MESSAGE

MAKING IT WORK: REACHING UNCHURCHED TEENS

★ Describe the most meaningful thing an adult (other than a family member) did for you or with you when you were a teenager. How could something like that be an outreach action in your ministry?

★ What do you personally do that seems to interest and attract teens? What could be done to spice up interactions with teens even more in your ministry?

★ How would you prepare for an influx of new unchurched teens? What would you change? What would you keep the same?

RAVES ABOUT RICK

Rick Bundschuh was sentenced to spend his life on the remote island of Kauai, Hawaii, a little more than twenty-three years ago. His crime was several decades of youth ministry.

Eventually, Rick decided he should do something a bit more profitable on the island other than surfing every day, and that's when he started writing lots of books, doing cartoon illustrations, working with teens and with some friends, and starting a church that people who don't much like going to church would enjoy. (They called it Kauai Christian Fellowship, which sounded quite clever at the time.) The rest of the time Rick tries to be a good husband to Lauren. He is almost done raising four kids, and a weenie dog is still around. (He plans to keep the wife and dog but kick the last kid out when he turns eighteen.) Rick, his family, and a quiver of surfboards make their home in Poipu, Kauai.

NOTES

Y★UTH MINISTRY IN THE TRENCHES

Engaging & Inspiring Youth Ministry Reading

Filled with practical ideas, these youth ministry books are "return-to" resources written in an easy-to-read style. Our featured authors—Marv Penner, Wayne Rice, and Rick Bundschuh— have more than a half-century of youth ministry experience in the trenches!

Reaching Unchurched Teens
remains an area of confusion and difficulty—even anxiety—for many youth leaders who want to provide their students with practical tools for reaching their friends who don't know Christ.

Building & Mobilizing Teams
is a critical need at a time when many leaders feel the need for more help, the necesity of delegating, and the importance of highly involved volunteers who care deeply for students.

Engaging Parents as Allies
—making sure they're involved and feel needed—is critical as youth ministry continues to evolve. Many leaders are experiencing an increasing need to involve parents in ministry—not push them away.

Standard®
P U B L I S H I N G